Stories

QUIET COURAGE

by Mary Jane Nordgren, D.O.

Cover by William A. Helwig

QUIET COURAGE is a collection of stories too human to be fiction dedicated to:

Earl, Kathi, Alisa, Ted, Bill, Adam, Amy, Chuck, Cathi, Betty, Pride, Jo, Jane, Lita, Pam, Virginia and so many others who deal with life's sometimes terrible ironies with heroic courage and grace. Their stories are told with respect, just as they were given to me or disguised for their comfort.

ISBN 0-9703896-2-0

Copyright 2004
By Mary Jane Nordgren, D.O.
and William A. Helwig
All rights reserved

Printed in the U.S.A. by Morris Publishing
3212 E. Hwy 30
Kearney NE 68847
800- 650-7888

QUIET COURAGE

by Mary Jane Nordgren, D.O.

QUIET COURAGE

Stories Too Human to be Fiction

Table of Contents

TOW	5
WOLVES at the DOOR	12
TILLER	19
YOURS, MINE, OURS, HOMEGROWN and STORE BOUGHT	26
BROTHERLY LOVE	31
DISTRACTION	33
SIGN of the TIMES	37
YOU'RE TOAST	39
GUMMING IT UP	43
HOSANNA	47
BRIAN'S INSIGHT	48
LADDER UPWARDS	54
ANGRY TEEN ANGEL	59
NIGHT BAG	67
ON the SPOT	76
OVERWHELMED	78
SHARE	85
JO	92
ENEMY ID	99
GRINDING DOWN	105

Table of Contents

MILLIE'S FIGHT	110
ALPINE WW II	115
SADIE	122
SELMA	128
BEGGIN' STRIP	132
FOOTLESS in SPOKANE	136
BRIDGE to the FUTURE	140
SMOKIN' CRADLE	146
BABE of the WOODS	149
LOG ROLL	153
HOME PLACE	155
BIG FOOT DEL	157
PASSAGE	163
TATTERED	169
The COURAGE of HOPE	172
GERRY DANCERS	176
T ROSES *	181

* T ROSES is reprinted thanks to A CUP OF COMFORT FOR WOMEN, Adams Media Corp

TOW

'It's okay, Mom,' Marty said into the pay phone, 'we know about the storm. Hell, there's always a storm up here in Alas...'

Marty held the receiver away from his ear and shrugged his ten-year-old shoulders. He loved the ripe language among the Alaska fishermen, but he'd forgotten his mother back in Oregon didn't yet know how much of a man he'd become in these last seven weeks on his father's boat.

'Mom, I'm sorry, I gotta go. It's almost dawn and Pa is... Yeah, sure, of course I'll take care of him. You should see my muscles now, Mom... Yeah, we're eating just fine. I'll take care... What? Oh, okay, I will. Bye, Mom. We'll call when we get back, promise.'

Marty was running almost before he'd hung up the phone. He'd heard the anxiety in his mother's voice and he'd promised to hug his father for her, but he hadn't said when or where, and it sure wasn't going to be here on the docks now with all the fishing crews getting underway. Moms!

'Everything all right at home?' Vernon called as Marty cast off the lines and jumped on board. Vern had watched his son leaping down the stairs two at a time and dashing across the dock. Time was when just the uneven roll of the dock under his feet would have sent him chumming. Marty was small yet for ten, but the way he'd pitched in to help on this boat Marian's Uncle Peter had willed them, well, Vern was as proud of his oldest boy as he was hopeful that the boat would prove itself this summer. Marian had been reluctant to let him try.

'One summer,' Vern had pleaded. 'If we don't make it pay, then we can decide, but at least we'll know what we're really dealing with,' he'd said and she'd finally stopped protesting, though she never was truly in favor. 'Who knows, Hon, it might go so good we can dump our jobs at the cannery and move up there. It would be a great place to raise the three kids, with all outdoors like that.'

'In the winter?' she'd said with raised eyebrows. 'If you want to fish so bad, why don't you take it out over the Columbia bar and fish here? At least then I'd see you every few days or weeks.'

'Because the boat's up there in Alaska, licensed and ready to go. Besides, they say the fishing up there is so huge that you can make $10,000 in a month!'

'Uncle Peter also said there are a lot more men maimed and drowned up there than we ever hear of in our Oregon papers,' Marian shot back, brown eyes blazing. 'What am I supposed to do if you go wracking yourself up? And you want to take Marty along?'

'He'll never learn any younger,' Vern had smiled.

'And he may never get any older!' she'd snapped and refused to speak to him again for two days. But in the end the boy prevailed. He wanted so badly to prove himself with his pa.

'Yeah, everything's okay at home,' Marty explained as the Pitchin' Peter eased away from the dock. 'Mom'd just heard about a storm coming in from the Bering Straight and she thought maybe we'd stay in today.'

'Did you remind her that we check Weather every morning before we leave?' Vern spun the wheel to head across the bay.

'Yeah, I told her, but she already knew that. Women,' Marty snarled and, hearing his father laugh out loud, looked up to be sure he wasn't the butt of whatever the joke was.

'You're growing up, Son,' Vern said gently. 'Maybe a little too fast up here. But you're holding your own,' he added and turned away to steer into the channel.

Marty's skinny chest swelled with pride. All the chumming, all the bruises and cuts and hours of working way past exhaustion - all of the tough times meant nothing once his father said that. Marty was even enough of a young man to say not a word in response. Instead, he sidled to the stern to sort out and stow the boxes they'd lugged on board this morning before he'd been called up to answer the pay phone in front of the Agua Mariner.

'Women,' he muttered again, thinking of how embarrassed he'd been when Old Felix had hollered out for all the fishing fleet to hear, 'Dannison! It's your old lady!' It wasn't until three boxes later, though, that Marty remembered to swear. This world of men wasn't easy to work your way into. There was a lot of important stuff to remember.

By 9:30 they'd hauled in and iced more than a third of the hold. And then the fish just disappeared. Gone. Marty could count on his fingers the decent fish they were seeing with each trap. Worse, the wind was picking up. The swells were lifting so even with his hard-earned seven-week sea legs, Marty was beginning to feel as green as the tinge of color suffusing through the gathering clouds. He glanced up at a bank of glaucous gray threatening from the northwest as his father hauled in the last of their traps and headed for the cabin. As

Marty coiled rope, the Pitchin' Peter turned west against the grain and fought its way farther out to sea.

'Marty!' Vern called out, and Marty hurried to the cabin. 'Listen to this,' Vern said, pointing to the speaker for their all-valuable radio. 'Can you make anything of all that?' But Uncle Peter hadn't believed much in the new-fangled gear, and the radio was older than Marty. It didn't work well this far out.

'We need that new antenna,' Marty commented and his father nodded. They did, but it was only one in a whole list of things they needed.

'Seen them clouds?'

Marty nodded.

'That may be a warning on the squawk box. You want we should turn back to port?'

Marty peered at Vernon's face. Marty was afraid, but there was no way he was going to admit that to this father who had just admitted him into the realm of men.

'It's up to you, Pa,' he said finally.

The pride that crept into Vernon's eyes more than made up for whatever qualms Marty had felt. His mother had reminded just this morning that his father was no quitter and sometimes that got him into trouble.

'You'll have to be the sensible one sometimes, Son,' she'd said. But that was an unfair burden, and Marty knew he'd rather die with his pa than appear the child or the coward in his father's eyes ever again.

'I'm with you,' Marty said low.

'Good,' Vernon responded. 'Then we'll head out maybe another ten miles and if it gets worse or there's still no fish, then we'll talk again and think about heading back. That okay with you?'

Was it ever! For the first time in his young life, Marty had been consulted in a decision between men. Stuffing his hands deep into the pockets of his jeans, Marty worked to control the vigor of his nod of assent.

'Better get out there and lash everything down the best you can, then. I've got a feeling it's gonna be a rough one.'

Marty hauled on his heavy weather jacket and buckled it midway. The rains had started for certain while he was in the shelter of the cabin.

'Try the hat,' Vern told him as he was about to head out on deck. 'Wish your mother could see you in that thing.'

Marty laughed, and heard his father's chuckle as he went out into the growing storm. The waves were higher, so high in fact that the ten-year-old could picture them sweeping him off the deck and into the roiling water without his being strong enough to fight to stay aboard. Then what would his pa do? There were only the two of them on the Pitchin' Peter and the little vessel, sturdy as it was, was indeed living up to its name. Great Uncle Peter must have known weather like this, and he made it. So would Marty and his father. They'd prove to everyone that they could do this. It was a good way to earn their living. Ma would see. Maybe they would bring the kids up here to Alaska. Marty grinned against the sting of salt water and rain as he pictured himself showing them the ropes.

Speaking of ropes, Marty'd heard old Felix talk about how much harder it is to twist and knot a rope when it was cold and wet. Now Marty believed him in muscle and wrenched gut as well as mind. He wasn't even half way done with the lashing down when the wind turned so ferocious, it picked up the Peter and hurled it down the trough of a thirty-foot sneaker wave. Marty didn't even have time to suck air. He clung to the rope and was battered like a mouse being toyed with by a malicious cat.

Then the Peter went still. Marty could no longer hear the engine or feel its throb under his feet.

The rest wasn't so much something he experienced as that he hung on and survived. Marty was aware of flood after flood of bone-chilling water washing over him and carrying him across the deck that slanted first one way and then another. He hit his head. He saw stars in the fuming gray, though his eyes were tightly closed. His legs flailed. His arms stiffened. His hands were no longer

9

his own but now a frozen part of the rope he gripped with terror for his life.

And then a strong hand grabbed the rope, nearly tearing it from his hands. But his father's other arm encircled his waist and drew him against the stalwart body. For the first time in what had seemed like hours, Marty remembered warmth and security. He was safe. His father had him. But his hands refused to let go of the rope even then.

Vernon flew with his son across the stern of the little fishing boat, and was smashed with him back onto the deck. In the single instant that the Pitchin' Peter steadied, Vern heaved with all his strength to propel them toward the mast.

He was talking to the boy, telling him he'd secure him so he wouldn't be washed overboard - as half or more of their equipment had been, even much of what Marty had tried with his limited strength to lash down.

The next wave sent the Peter slithering, careening, and Vernon crushed his son between his own chest and the mast, holding on for both of them. Cascades drummed over them. Vern held on. He could feel the boy going limp in his arms.

At the next respite, Vern took up the slack of the rope Marty still clung to and lashed his reeling son to the mast. And then they were plummeting again, and Vern held on for everything he was worth. He hadn't knotted the boy tight yet. He had to cling there, calling on strength born of adrenaline and a parent's desperate love.

How long he struggled to secure his son, he couldn't have told you. But it was wave after wave before he was sure the boy wouldn't go down unless the boat did.

With the boy half-dazed but secure, Vern fought his way to the stern to open the cover to do what he could to work on the motor. He knew cars. He only hoped he could guess at boats.

And then what he had not dared pray for happened: human voices. Close.

Vernon lifted his head against the storm. Through the sting of wind and water, Vern could see another fishing vessel, with Norwegian flag furled and unfurled in dizzying rapidity, coming up alongside. A tall, fair-haired giant of a man yelled through huge, cupped hands.
'Do you vant a tow?'

Marty sat huddled in dry blankets in the corner booth at the Aqua Mariner, sipping steaming coffee from a mug his bandaged hands could barely hold. Mostly he hunched over the rising vapor and let its warmth and aroma bathe his nose and chin. He looked up when his father came back and slid into the booth on the opposite side of the laminated table.
'Whadya tell Mom?' Marty asked.
'Not much. Just that we're back and okay. She was glad to hear my voice.'
'Did she scold?'
'For what? She got what she wanted: news that I've sold the Peter.'

Marty's jaw dropped dangerously close the hot coffee. 'Sold?' he stammered, but he knew the why, so he clamped his mouth and didn't ask. Nor did he have to tell his father he was sorry - and glad. They were friends now. Whatever they found to do back in Oregon, Marty would find a way to help out. The dreams of life in Alaska were just that - dreams. The little kids, even Mom, would have had a real tough go trying to make it up here.

Vern nodded, as though they'd exchanged all that in spoken conversation.

'Those Norwegian fishermen, Pa. I didn't get to thank them for towing us in. Where are they?'

Vernon's lip split and bled again as he opened his mouth in a guffaw. 'Oh, Marty, how to tell you? They unhooked the Pitchin' Peter, saw me onto the dock with you in my arms, saluted and went back out into that storm.'

'Back into that storm?'

'Yeah, they said they hadn't finished fishing yet.'

WOLVES AT THE DOOR

Kay steeled herself to open the last of the nasty letters. She glanced at the rain against the picture window at the end of their living room, remembering how delighted they'd been when they first saw it with the realtor. Even with the trees in the front yard giving them some privacy, they'd thought, the sunshine would bathe this room in warmth and joy.

To be honest, for a while it had. Laughter rang throughout this little ranch house in the suburbs south of town. Tinkling giggles from Ali; deep chuckles from Chip; booming laughter from Bud's huge chest. And joy in Kay's heart as she stood in the doorway of the kitchen looking at her husband's size sixteen shoes beside their children's tiny sandals under the dining room table and listening to their bantering over a game of Chutes and Ladders. How good Bud had always been with the babies. They seemed even tinier than they were against his enormous frame. He had a way of soothing them, making them feel protected. What could harm them in such gentle, muscular arms?

They'd just bought this house (with the bank's help) when the vet clinic came available. If they'd known it was coming, they'd never have stretched so far as to try to buy a house, too. But there it was, and Bud and Kay looked at each other, took a deep breath and said, 'We can do this.'

As a new veterinarian, Kay was full of ideas and enthusiasm, but she had little practical business experience. As always with a new small business, they were a while getting out of red ink.

That first month of black ink was cause for celebration!

The next month was catastrophic. If only it had been a disaster to the clinic, Kay thought, it would just have been money.

But Bud, groaning, had gotten up in the middle of one Friday night. When he didn't come back to bed, Kay slipped on her robe and searched their new house in the dark. She found him on the couch in the living room, staring at the picture window.

When she touched him, he groaned.

'What is it, Honey?' she asked.

'My head,' he moaned. And then he'd gone into seizures.

The 9-1-1 dispatcher was both competent and compassionate. Kay would always be grateful for that assuring voice that told her an ambulance was on its way.

Kay called her mom. She answered in a voice groggy with sleep that she could make it to them in just over an hour. She'd check at the hospital first, since it was on

13

her way. No matter what it was, she'd be there to help with the kids, at least.

When the ambulance arrived, the paramedics were visibly relieved that Bud had come out of his seizure and was again able to sit up and talk. They were even more relieved that he was able to stand and walk with them to the ambulance. His three hundred-pound frame would have been difficult to carry.

The whole family rallied around, from all their distance. But Bud and Kay alone had to make the decision about surgery. It was a brain tumor, and it would continue to grow.

'It's okay. We just signed the papers and the agent said there'd be no problem getting the insurance. Boy, I'm glad we signed up when we did,' Bud smiled.

But it wasn't so. The agent's verbal assurance notwithstanding, they got a rejection letter in the mail on Wednesday. It was dated the afternoon of the Friday their world had come apart. Their attorney said there was nothing they could do except demand their initial deposit check be returned.

So they were doing the surgery without insurance, and with too much income and too many assets for help from the state. They worked out a payment plan with the hospital and doctors, and bit their lips and scheduled the surgery.

The insistent letters from the ambulance company and the utility and vet supply companies started coming even before Bud entered pre-op.

And now Bud lay with his head swathed in bandages. The surgery had gone pretty well. The surgeons were able to get the bulk of it, but dared not probe further into the structure of his brain. Bud would be on anti-convulsant medications for an undetermined length of time. And they cost money, too.

Kay took the children with her to the clinic. They could no longer afford daycare. The clinic was set up in her name, but somehow the bill collectors found the connection and began calling her at work as well as home. She dreaded the ringing of the phone even though it was more likely to be a patient than a bill collector.

Bud recovered from the surgery, but he no longer played much with the kids. His depression clouded his once smiling face. The children cowered where once they had stepped forward with enthusiastic questions.

They cut back expenses as best they could. Kay did more of the scut work herself rather than hire the new technician they sorely needed, but that meant she was paying with her own health. There wasn't much time for sleep, even if she could have rested in the worrisome night.

Family helped where they could with work hours and with money, but the pile of bills and vicious letters grew every month. And the phone calls. Those were the hardest to deal with. Some came at midnight or after. What could she tell them at one or two A.M. that she couldn't tell them during the day? What did those harassing calls accomplish except to rob them of needed recuperation?

Kay opened the last of today's pile of unwelcome mail. She flopped onto the couch and stared at the rain on the window, too numb even to be angry.

'We're going to lose the cars, and the house, and probably the clinic,' she said out loud. It was terrifying to hear the words she'd been dreading. But then, somehow, it was relieving, as well.

There, it's been said right out loud, she thought. She'd faced it. If it was true, and it well could be, then what? This rainy afternoon at home was the first time she'd been able to think past the dread.

Then what? Bud is alive and gaining strength. He could still draw incredible pictures and he'd worried most about losing his artist's skill. She had training that no one could take away from her. She could find work with another veterinarian. They'd eat. And they'd repay. Or, if they had to go into bankruptcy, she'd at least be able to earn enough to keep them in an apartment and eating mac and cheese. They were down, that was for sure. But there weren't out.

Kay sat up, facing the window and the rain. 'All right. You can take my home and my clinic, if that's what you want. But you aren't going to destroy my family.' Her lips tightened in determination, but the decision being made, she was as relieved as the ambulance personnel had been.

For the first time in months, Kay chuckled as she remembered their faces. She let out a deep breath and let her chin drop. It was going to be all right. They weren't defeated. She wouldn't let them be.

She must have napped. She was surprised to hear the front door open and Chip come slouching in.

'Hi, Honey,' she called, not quite awake. 'Where's Ali?'

'She's over at Munsons'. Don't you remember you said she could go?'

'Oh. Yeah. Well, and how are you, my big boy?' She tried to take him into her lap, but he almost wiggled away after their big hug. 'What's the matter, Hon?'

'Dad,' he mumbled.

'What about Dad?'

'Monster.'

'What?' Kay sat up. 'Monster? Your dad? I don't think so.'

'He's so big.'

'Yes, he is that.'

'He's almost a giant.'

Kay smiled. 'Pretty close.'

Chip twisted in her arms, but she drew him closer. When he wouldn't say anything more, she held him tight against her and stroked his cheek.

'What made you think about giants, Chipper?'

'The librarian read about them at story hour,' he muttered finally, but just that much seemed to open the floodgates. He talked about the session in the library and how everybody hated the ogre and how all giants were ogres and his father was a giant so he must be a monster, too.

Kay held him, listening to the child's fears behind the story and his terror at the breaking-up of his home and the worry of his parents.

'It's all right,' she murmured over and over as she let him unburden what he'd accumulated through these frightening months.

And she felt her own emotions in reaction to his words. Anger: How could you say a thing like that about your own father? But that would lead to her little boy's feeling guilty. Despair: How could he add to her burden when she had so much against her already? But how could he know what they were really dealing with? And why should anyone this young have to help deal with what were adult problems? Heartsick, she held him close and rocked him.

But she'd made a decision. And in that moment Kay was glad he'd come home when he did and not an hour sooner. The decision was made. She knew what she was willing to give up and what she wasn't. Not for the life of her was she about to tear any deeper into this family. Instead, she realized what was really happening here.

'Honey, aren't you mixing things up?'

'What?' Chip was curious. The fear was already receding as he'd been allowed to vent it. 'Mixing what up?'

'Weren't those stories about the ogres and the giants?'

'Yeah,' Chip sat up in her arms and turned to face her.

'And isn't Daddy a person, a real live person?'

'Yeah.'

'So aren't you mixing up...'

'I know! Just because Daddy is big, that doesn't mean he's a monster. I'm mixing up real stuff and stories.' He grinned.

'Fact and fiction,' she smiled back. 'A lot of us get mixed up that way. For a while, anyway.' Kay hugged him until in a few minutes he kissed her nose and hopped down.

'Do we got any bread? I'd like some cinnamon toast, I think.'

Kay rose, glancing at the beautiful patterns of rain on the window. 'I think we can come up with that. And how about some hot chocolate?'

'With marshmallows?'

'Sure, if we have any.' They did. Stale and a little hard, but they melted in the steaming cocoa. Kay and Chip sat in the warmth of the kitchen and laughed, despite the rain.

TILLER ⌘

Den had a little brother, but he could barely walk on uneven ground, let alone reach the pedals. But just to be sure, Den sweated to hoist him up enough for Biff to scramble over fenders and gears to haul himself up onto the seat. Biff settled in the scooped metal, half of which was too wide for his little bottom. Biff was sitting over and in front of tines that would have halved his little body. He was crawling among gears that could have jarred loose, lurching the tiller and throwing him. But neither the two-and-a-half year old nor the five-year-old worried. They were little men - little farmers.

'Well, stretch down,' Den ordered, disgusted that his baby brother wasn't even getting halfway to the pedals.

'I'm are!' Biff wailed and burst into tears that streaked his dusty cheeks.

'Oh, well, if you're going to cry about it,' Den stuffed his fists inside the bib of his overalls. If Mama found out what they were up to, she'd lay into him for not using better sense in taking care of his baby brother. 'Baby' was right. Sometimes the kid was purely a pain in the neck.

Biff's chin was quivering, a sure sign that he was about to howl. That would bring Mama running.

'Well, come on down then,' Den growled. He almost called him 'Baby,' but the insult would surely bring the howl - and Mama. And Dennis didn't want anyone to know yet what he was up to. Not until he had found a way to make it work. Any farmer worth his salt figured things out for himself. Papa had said that often enough, and Papa was right about just about everything.

'It's okay, Biffer,' Den crooned. He wiggled in between the housing and the wheel and raised his arms to his little brother. 'Come on, old son, I'll catch you.'

It was a testimonial to faith and trust that the little guy launched himself out over the equipment into his brother's arms. They landed in a heap in front of the huge tractor wheel, but Biff stood up and shook himself, laughing.

'Yeah, that was a whole lot of fun,' Den sneered from underneath. 'Yeah, I guess it was,' he agreed when he got up and checked. Nothing more serious than a few new scrapes. Scrapes and bruises were so much a part of farm life that neither boy noticed them any more.

Biff hung his head.

'Ah, don't worry, Biffer,' Den told him, pulling out his shirttail to wipe the little one's eyes where the dust threatened to drop in from his sun-bleached eyebrows. 'You'll get bigger enough to reach them pedals for me. Maybe next year. It's okay. I ain't really tried to steer and work them pedals myself yet. Just thought you'd like to help, that's all. Yeah, sure, I can probably do it just fine by myself. You just stand over there by the fence and watch me. Keep an eye out for me, will ya? We don't want nobody squealing to Papa until we see if we can get this garden tilled for him. Won't he be surprised? Yeah, over there. You be my lookout, will ya, Biff? Thanks.'

With the little fellow safely out of the way and happy to be helping, Den clambered up into the tractor seat. He scooched forward as far as he could, but the pedals were beyond reach of his feet, too.

'Gotta be a way,' he muttered. But there was no way to lower the seat that he could discover. 'So why do I got to be sitting in the seat?' he asked himself finally. The men sat because it was almost comfortable when they worked the tractor hour after hour, day after day. But there was no law said you had to work it from the seat. No reason why a strong boy couldn't stand on the center bar and run the gears and the pedals and the steering wheel from standing up.

'All clear?' Den yelled to Biff to keep him occupied. Den from his height could see better than Biff could that no one was paying the least bit of attention to them.

'Yeah, Den!' Biff called back. 'Go!'

Den took one more glance around, then turned the key. The old engine protested a little, then caught and settled into a chugging that promised to keep going all day long, despite heat and dust.

'Yea,' Biff seemed to cheer, but Den couldn't be sure over the sound of the motor.

'Okay,' Den said to himself, 'here goes!' He ran over emergency procedures quickly in his mind, then slid the gear lever over two notches and felt the tractor lunge forward. It took his whole strength on the steering wheel to hang on.

'Too much gas. You're not out to beat anybody but the weather and the elements,' Papa's admonition echoed in Den's mind. It wasn't the fastest guy who won at farming, but the steadiest. When he'd balanced himself against the front of the seat in the best position, he slid the gear lever over another notch for power rather than speed. And then he slowly lifted his foot from the brake. The tractor hauled forward again, more controllably this time.

'Yea!' Biff was cheering. Den grinned. He hadn't been at all sure this would work.

With some experience behind him in driving the tractor - from Dad's lap - Den steered toward the near corner of the two-acre garden patch. He knew how to stop when he straddled the edge row. Biff came running, but Den waved him back. He wasn't sure enough yet to risk letting his little brother ride up behind him on the seat. Better to get a couple furrows under his own belt first. Or under his overall straps, he chuckled.

'You keep an eye out, you hear?' Den called. 'Somebody might just hear the motor and come out to check.'

He climbed up onto the seat with the lever out of gear to be sure the tiller was lined up right behind him. If he was going to till this field, he'd better get it right or his mistake would be there for all to see for the whole season. It was okay. He'd steered okay. Now to work the handle lever to lower the tines to the ground. The forward motion of the tractor pulling would dig the pointed blades into the earth as they went.

The handle went hard. It was supposed to. That was to keep kids from being able to do things they weren't yet old enough or strong enough to do. But Den was five, and Den was determined. He wrestled with it until the blades were poised and ready to chew up the ground for Mama's family-feeding vegetable garden.

Den grinned as he pictured Mama's face. She had such a pretty smile when she was pleased.

And Papa would be proud. Den set his mouth. Den would do this right, so Papa would have to be proud.

With a last, conspiratorial wave at Biff, Den lowered himself over the pedals again and slid the gear lever over. They hitched forward, the tines jostled, then bit, and they were tilling. Den was actually tilling the farm. On his own. With no one to show him how or tell him what to do. Den was farming. He'd never felt so much like a man in his whole life.

It went well, slowly, but fairly straight and just the right depth, the way Mama liked it. Den took the chance near the end of the first row to let one hand off the steering wheel to wipe his dripping brow and the dust out of his eyes. He was coming to the end of the line of furrows. This was going to be the hard part.

The trick was to lift the tiller and swing the tractor in a tight a half-circle to avoid the fence. Then he had to line up for the furrows going back the other way. Doing that many maneuvers at one time wasn't a cinch for Rudy or even for Papa. Den wasn't at all sure he could do it, but he was pretty darn sure he couldn't do it all in one motion.

At the end of the row, Den stopped and clambered back up onto the seat to maneuver the handle and lift the tines. Maybe when he was sure of himself he could make the turn with them down, but right now he wanted to be able to move the tractor back and forth if he had to. If he hit that fence, all the good he was trying to do would be lost. Papa would see only the damage.

With the tiller up, Den balanced on his feet again, and slowly, cautiously, set the gears to inch forward.

That second row, he had to back up once, but only a little way. Maybe next swing he'd be able to do it in just one motion. But the steering wheel pulled hard. Real hard. Den was sweating something fierce by the time he got that tractor lined up to where he could lower the tines. He yanked his shirttail out as much as it would go and wiped his face. The shirt fell away grimy. Mama wouldn't be pleased. But maybe she wouldn't mind once she saw her garden ready.

Den lowered the tines and slid forward to stand up. The balancing was easier this time. The sweep at the end of the row was easier because the fence was a ways back and by the second time Den came that way, he was ready to try making the turn without raising the tines.

Along about the middle of the fifth row, he slid the gear lever over a notch and, at least on the straightaway, picked up the chugging pace.

Den was so engrossed in his self-appointed chore that he forgot about his brother.

Biff had stood guard valiantly. He'd cheered for the rows and the turns seven times before he admitted that Den wasn't waving back, wasn't even looking over at him. At two-and-a-half, this was taking too long and Biff smelled the newmade bread fresh from Mama's oven. He toddled to the farmhouse, alone.

'Where's your brother?' Mama demanded as she handed him a heel slathered with butter.

His mind engrossed in eating, Biff told before he remembered he was guarding the secret.

Mama stared at him. 'Tilling?' she asked, nearly breathless. 'He's five years old! What is your father thinking? Stay here, young man.' When Mama ordered in that voice, Biff lowered his bread and gaped at her, but he didn't dare go farther than the porch door to watch.

Mama tore off across the back yard to the barn. Pretty soon Papa raced out of the barn with Rudy lumbering behind him and Mama, her apron up near her face, scurrying behind Rudy. Mama only raised that apron to wipe sweat - or to cry.

Biff watched the men running with their arms raised, straight into the garden. Biff could see Papa leap onto the tractor. It stopped a whole lot faster with Papa treading on the brakes than it ever had with Den standing on them.

And then Papa climbed down with Den on his shoulder. Rudy scrambled up into the seat and worked the rows while Papa carried Den back toward the house with Mama clinging to his arm and reaching up to stroke Den's leg and his back.

Mama was laughing and crying.

Papa was grinning. 'Now Mama, the boy's going on six this fall. He done what was needed and he done it good. How about some bread and that last blackberry preserves you been saving for a hungry farmer?'

At last Den looked at his little brother. Den, with his chin high and his smile so wide he looked in danger of busting open.

'Biff helped, Papa,' Den said as he was lowered to the porch floor. 'Biff was look-out, and he done good. We got near the whole upper acre done before anybody found us.'

Mama drew her younger boy close. 'You both done good,' she murmured. Never would she tell how she'd found out about the famous garden tilling operation.

To Dennis Johnson

YOURS, MINE, OURS, HOMEGROWN and STORE-BOUGHT ✌

'I warned him,' Sharon said, tossing her soft dark hair. 'Before we were married, I told him, "There are three things you'd better know about me:

'Number 1. I break electrical appliances. Hey, with our big family, we're likely to run through a couple washers and dryers before our tenth anniversary. I've had to replace five toasters and three industrial-strength, heavy-duty food mixers. Light bulbs burn out when I walk into the room. So, Bill, be sure you figure that in your budget. We're going to need way more appliances than you'd ever think possible."

Bill's long face crinkled in a growing smile. This dynamo of a little wife-to-be was so intense, so sincere, saying things that, even if they were true, were expenses he could live with. Sharon was definitely worth a whole new set of appliances every year, if that's what it took.

'Okay,' he told her. Laconic to her loquacious, Bill nodded for her to go on.

'Well, then, number 2. Remember the "Patty Duke Show" where she gets all these wild ideas and schemes and plunges into them and then needs to be rescued? That's me. I'm Patty Duke. I do that. I won't try to make you miserable on purpose, but you'd better be ready to deal with some far-out projects that sounded perfectly reasonable when I thought of them.'

His eyebrows raised a little on that one.

'Oh, I'll always ask you about them first,' Sharon added.

He shook his head. He'd never been able to say 'No' to her and doubted that he ever would. It scared him a little. He'd never been all that mechanically minded, but if that's what she needed, he'd try.

'Okay,' he agreed, then swallowed. These two he could deal with, but he had the feeling the third thing she felt he needed to know about her was going to be a whopper.

It was.

'Bill, you know how some people collect stamps?'

'Yes.'

'And some people collect Tobey pitchers?'

'Uh-huh.'

'And some other people collect figurines?'

Bill squared his shoulders. 'Just what is it you collect, Sharon?'

'Children,' she murmured with her head cocked to one side. She was looking at him with that Take-It-Or-Leave-Me kind of expression that showed her pain at the thought of his rejection.

He nearly laughed. 'Children? You're serious?'

'Oh, yes, about children, I am,' she told him with an earnestness he could not ignore. 'I've always wanted a dozen of my own and probably a full complement of foster kids.'

'Oh?' The single word was all he could express. His eyebrows rose on their own. She couldn't be serious? Two dozen children? Twenty-four mouths to feed and heads to shelter? Forty-eight feet to keep on the right path? Bill gulped, finally aware that Sharon was still speaking.

'You must love kids, too. You are so good to your own Sally and Steven.'

'I love them, yes,' he agreed.

'And you'll want them to live with us?'

'I - yes, I'd want that. With all my heart, if you'll have them.'

'Of course!' she cried, hugging him. 'I'd love to have them with us. And my three - almost four.'

His eyebrows shot up again. 'Are you telling me you're expecting?'

'Oh, no, no,' she laughed. 'Not yet. We're not married yet, you know.' She wagged a finger at him.

'But you said, 'Almost four.''

'Well, my brother's daughter, April. She's so sweet, and her mom is in such a straight since my brother's gone. I'd like to tell April that she's always welcome to be with us, whenever she needs us or even whenever she'd like.'

'Oh,' Bill managed again. 'I guess - I guess, sure, that'd be okay. If she has need...'

'So that's five, maybe six. I want you to get to know my three.'

'Well, I've seen Cher and Robbie. And you've talked about Danny, but he's always been somewhere else so I haven't seen him...'

'He's Black, you know. Adopted. He laughs when I tell him he's 'store-bought.' Through that international agency,' Sharon screwed up her pretty mouth. 'When it took so long for me to have another one after Cher - there's seven years between her and Robbie, you know - I decided we may as well adopt. So I went through Holtz, is it? I asked for a boy for my first husband. He'd fought in the Korean War and his family hadn't had much experience with Negroes, so there were a couple of complete no-nos.'

'And Danny is not only Black, he's part Korean, I take it,' Bill finished, his eyebrows again betraying his feelings.

'As a matter of fact, yes. His mother was Korean and his father was a Black GI,' she smiled.

'And Rob and his parents?'

'They loved him. Or, if they didn't, they never let him know.'

'That's pretty courageous,' Bill said.

'It took me a while to realize I'd have to work differently with him. I always thought there was one clear way that was best for parenting, but I've since learned you give foundations that are firm, but you work with each kid's needs. Tailor-made. Robbie was someone again from the other two. And if April comes, then she's is going to be even more different. I don't know Sally and Steve well enough yet to know what they'll need. I'm going to have to follow your lead for a while, I imagine. And we'll talk.'

Bill pressed his palms and lifted them to touch his upper lip with the tips of his index fingers.

'You are a wonder, Sharon,' he whispered.

She started toward him, then stopped, realizing the decision was now his and she had no right to interfere one way or the other, despite her longing.

When his silence strung out minute after minute, Sharon shrank back.

'And now you're beginning to wonder?' she asked, so quietly.

His eyebrows lifted slightly as though he was startled.

'Me? Wondering? About what?'

'About taking on a lady who blows out light bulbs,' she murmured.

'Oh, that,' he waved a hand dismissively. 'No, I was just imagining what it will be like with five or six kids.'

Her shoulders lowered. She hadn't realized how tense she'd been, waiting for her love to reject her.

'Or more?' she asked, rushing to him.

He took her in his arms, but his eyes widened. 'More?'

'If we should have one or two of our own?'

'One or two?' Bill laughs now. 'We had four of 'ours.' Joe, Emily, Matthew and Jacob. Don't know what we'd do without any one of them. Can't even imagine the world without all of them.' He gathers her into his arms and she leans her dark hair, now with individual strands of gray, against his chest. 'Hers, mine, all ours. Some store-bought. All homegrown whenever we can gather them home. Ten kids. If you'd have told me that someday I'd have ten kids, I'd have told you that was as likely as my having to replace the washing machine again this year. And the food mixer. Uh-oh, that lamp bulb just burned out.'

Bill takes his wife by the chin and lifts it so he can look into her eyes. 'Sharon?'

She smiles sweetly. 'Have I told you about Renee?'

BROTHERLY LOVE ♥

While the second graders opened their brand new ring binders to copy the list from the board, Miss Nugent sat down at her desk. What a joy it was to watch their eager faces this first day of school.

Max Reiber looked so much like his two older brothers that Miss Nugent picked him out as soon as he walked in the door. Katie Gonzales was going to be a leader. She was already helping the little Amesworth boy sharpen his pencil with a finger-held tool she got from her desk.

Nugent's eye scanned the list. She was pretty sure of who most of the children were. So those two must be the Foster boys, Marvin and Conrad. Funny, they didn't look like twins to be in the same grade. She frowned. Maybe they were cousins. Getting out the list the principal had just handed her with the complete information for her class, she scanned for the street addresses and names of the parents of the two boys. Yes, both lived on Kingsley Street, both at the same street number.

Hmmm, and both had Larry and Gladys listed as parents, but their birthdays were three months apart.

31

Now how could that be?

Quietly, Miss Nugent called the two boys to her desk.

'Are you cousins?' she asked.

The redhead, Conrad, turned to Marvin. They both shook their heads. 'No, Miss Nugent, we're brothers.'

'Your birthday, Marvin, is in January?'

Marvin nodded, brushing back honey-brown bangs.

'And your birthday is the second of April, Conrad?'

The boy's freckles lit up with his grin of agreement.

'But you're brothers?'

'Oh,' said Conrad, grasping her dilemma. 'Oh, yeah, we're brothers, Miss Nugent. One of us is adopted, but we can never remember which one.'

DISTRACTION ☺

'I figured out Mom's secret of being so good with little kids,' Ann said, laughing.

Not only did her mother Alice have a child's unabashed sense of joy with the world's small delights, but she also truly did enjoy the kids' board games. She could play Candy Land with the little ones for hours and never once moan, 'Not this again.'

But that wasn't all. Alice Marie had learned early that one secret of pleasant relationships was to avoid confrontation. She could take anyone's mind off the source of potential conflict with her inevitable smile. Ann found it fun to watch her two brothers learn that they'd been had. Johnny was the oldest, but Ann was pretty close behind him, especially over the blue gills.

The kids loved to go fishing with Dad. He'd take them to the Oswego lake not far from their home near Portland, Oregon. They'd make a day of it, often bringing home two or three or even five small blue gills.

'Oh, look at all those fish you've caught!' Mom would exclaim from the doorway. She'd hurry outside to admire and praise, but somehow the kids never did get those blue gills actually inside the house.

'Can we have them for supper, Mom? Can we, please, huh?' the kids would cry.

'Well, now, we have dinner all planned already for tonight,' she'd answer with a frown of concentration. 'And tomorrow night's is planned, too, I'm afraid,' she'd add. And then her face would light up with that smile that said she had just thought of a solution. 'How about if I bring out some freezer bags, and we'll wrap those fish up real good and put them in the freezer until the very right time to use them?'

'Yea!' the kids would cry and dig in triple-bagging those blue gills and helping set them carefully into the freezer.

Ann finally realized that each time the kids brought home blue gills, John would smile over at Dad while she and little Steve were busy with Mom stuffing the fish into plastic sacks. And then it dawned on her: They never did find the 'very right time' and they never did have blue gills for dinner any more than those fish ever even got into Mom's clean kitchen except within layers and layers of plastic. Which was probably just as well, she found out as an adult. Blue gills are not the best tasting fish in any lake.

Watching Steve bundling those fish for the 'very right time,' Ann almost said something. She was just on the verge of blurting out how they never did eat those fish because by the time 'maybe next week' came around, the kids had forgotten all about them. And neither Dad nor Mom saw fit to remind them.

'Annie,' John cautioned with his finger to his pursed lips. She looked from her older brother to Mom, who smiled a warning look, nodding at Ann's baby brother. Alice gently shook her head.

'Oh,' Ann said and covered her mouth with her hand. She was in on the secret. But Steve was too little to figure it out yet. She grinned, glad to be counted as one of the big people in the family.

Steve was quite a bit younger. 'Forty or fifty years younger,' he would say. And sometimes when Johnny and Ann were too busy to include their baby brother in what they were doing, Steve would wander off to find Mom, usually in her fragrant kitchen.

'Mom, I'm bored,' he'd sigh.

'Oh, well, do you think you could help me peel a potato?' she'd ask, all seriousness, as though his efforts would certainly be a great help in her meal preparations.

'Sure!' Like a knight bravely entering the fray to rescue his lady fair, Steve climbed up on the chair she set in front of the sink and donned the apron (usually tied like a bib around his neck so he wouldn't trip over its length if they fastened it around his waist).

Mom helped him scrub a huge, gnarly Idaho potato and gouge out the little roots, then with due ceremony entrusted him with the potato peeler.

While she went on with mixing her homemade rolls, Steve stood earnestly paring that potato down to the size of a softball. 'Is this okay?' he asked.

'Well, that's pretty good, but maybe just a little bit smaller,' she answered.

So Steve turned the tuber over and over in his hand, dutifully peeling while the mass of brown and white strips grew in the sink.

Eventually he got it down to the size of a tennis ball and again asked if it was to her liking.

'Maybe just a little bit more, if you can,' she answered gently.

He got it down to the size of a golf ball and held it up again for her to inspect.

'What a fine job!' she praised. 'Now, why don't you go to your room and play for a while?'

He hopped down and she helped him remove the apron, gave him a pat and a hug and off he ran, perfectly content.

'I didn't know that Steve didn't see through that particular brand of distraction Mom had used on him, not until we were gathered at his house for a family celebration when he was in his twenties,' Ann said. 'His new bride Anne had offered to host us all.'

'Is there anything I can do to help, Hon?' Steve asked.

'Well, I'm a little behind so if you could peel the potatoes, that'd be great,' Anne told him.

'Sure!' he answered gallantly. He stood in front of their kitchen sink and scrubbed eight or ten large potatoes and gouged out the roots. And then he set to work with the peeler. The pile of parings grew in the sink. And grew. And grew. He'd whittled that first potato down to the size of a golf ball when Anne walked over.

'What are you doing?' she asked. When she saw all the parings in the sink she giggled, and then she laughed out loud. Her mom and Ann stepped over to see what all the fun was about, and they laughed, too. They had to.

Steve seemed just a little miffed at being made fun of. He'd just done what he'd always done for Mom, Ann remembered.

'My mother deceived me,' he told his sister when she explained.

'Distracted you, little brother,' Ann corrected gently, and Steve grinned, knowing it was so.

When Alice Marie arrived carrying her homemade rolls and traditional birthday cake, Ann helped Steve put the goodies aside, so they both could hug her, long and deeply. No wonder they both had such happy memories of childhood.

SIGN OF THE TIMES

Judy was a '60's activist. She couldn't help it. Her dad was a lawyer for the Unions in Chicago and protest was born and bred in her.

Judy was also a pacifist. But Judy was neither calm nor calming. Judy was a one of the fiery pacifists who'd knock you down and stand over your bloody head to tell you the evils of war.

I loved her. We'd been friends since we were lowly Freshmen in college. While I'm not exactly a wallflower, I definitely qualified in comparison. Me, the quiet one: That's a laugh! But I was, if Judy was within a two-mile radius.

She was bright, funny, irreverent and irrepressible. And yet she was conservative by nature. It was just that her stated and unflinching values were not what most of the young people around us had grown up on.

She was Scandinavian blond, blue-eyed, broad-shouldered and tenderly loved by a second-generation Norwegian even taller and blonder, though not quite so broad-shouldered. In fact, Olie was downright skinny, and awkward, but oh, so smart! When Olie got a scholarship to do graduate studies in Electrical Engineering at Purdue, we happened to be going to Lafayette, Indiana, too, for graduate work, so the friendship continued.

Olie and Judy adored their little blond Elle. When Judy went to join a protest march, she simply took her toddler along. Judy hefted her sign, 'NO MORE WAR' and joined the circling line of protesters. 'DOWN WITH WAR' and 'MAKE LOVE, NOT WAR' proclaimed the hand-made placards. The demonstrators - some gray-haired, some too young to be able to mouth the words of rallying songs with more than childish lisps - took over the block of park and garden in the center of Lafayette. Those too little to stay interested naturally gravitated toward each other to play while their mothers and dads and even grandparents continued their marching. Elle joined a group of slightly older youngsters at their game of rock toss. But they had been playing together a while before she came, and she was not graciously received.

In fact, only a few minutes later Elle burst into tears and ran for her mother. 'Mommy, Mommy,' she cried, 'that boy hit me.'

Judy bent down under a sign reading, 'THERE HAS TO BE A BETTER WAY' and did her no-nonsense consoling of her weeping offspring.

'Well, hit him back,' Judy said.

YOU'RE TOAST! ☠

As Tim gave the signal, the salesmen ran their fingers through their hair and straightened their sports coats. Mr. Aggarun ran the second biggest Volkswagen dealership in Ohio, Indiana and Illinois. He'd gotten that big because he attended to details, he'd let you know in that gruff bass voice. He wasn't an imposing man until he opened his mouth. And then, even when he spoke softly, you listened.

'He's driving the bus,' Tim declared.

'I swear I don't know why you think you can guess his mood by which model he drives in the morning,' Clint grumbled. 'He's driving the latest one turned in on trade, that's all. Anyway, this is way too early in the morning for me.'

'You complain about that every Saturday,' Tim whined.

'Hey, you two, don't start,' Dennis said. 'We have to have sales department meetings. Saturday has the biggest volume of walk-in traffic so we'd all want to be here anyway, so why not have the meeting on a day when we're all here instead of calling some guy in on his day off?' Dennis was the practical one - and the peacemaker.

'So why does it have to be eight in the morning?'

'Would you rather have it after the sales day and cut into your Saturday night?'

'All right, all right,' Clint moaned. 'And there is our illustrious boss, stalking around each and every car on the lot before he comes in. He does that every day.'

'He likes to stay on top of things,' Tim sided with Dennis.

Dennis sighed. 'You know, I don't know how he keeps going.'

'He does look disheveled,' Tim agreed. 'How can a man with every hair in place...'

'Yeah, both of them,' Clint laughed. 'Our balding pater.'

'He's sad,' Dennis said. 'You've never been married, have you, Clint?'

'Not that they haven't tried to corral me, but I've never let anybody that near.'

'Then you don't know what it's like to lose someone who has been your whole life. Aggarun and his wife were so close. And those two boys. They adored their mother. I don't know how Mr. Aggarun can come back into work so soon after her funeral.'

'I don't know how he expects to raise those two boys alone,' Tim said. 'What are they now? Eight and six?'

'Nine and seven, I think,' Dennis said, rising as their boss entered the side door. 'Good morning, Mr. A. Ready for the conference room? It's all set up, I believe.'

'Good morning, all. Yes, let's get this meeting under way. Doris,' he walked to the counter to talk with the receptionist, 'please hold all calls until after the meeting, will you?'

They filed in behind Aggarun and took their places around the oak table. Gene Whitman slipped in, skirting being late, as usual. Don and Herb were already seated.

Aggarun took his place at the head and the meeting began. Figures. Charts. Questions. Explanations and lame excuses. Suggestions. An occasion sharp assessment. Aggarun was in the middle of an observation none too flattering to Gene when the phone rang, startling them all.

Frowning, Aggarun lifted the receiver. 'Yes?'

'I'm sorry, Mr. Aggarun,' they could all hear Doris's voice clearly disturbed, 'I know you asked me to hold all calls, but it's your son on the line and he sounded stressed. Shall I put him through?'

'Barry?'

'No, I believe it's the older one, Martin, isn't it?'

'Put him through.' Aggarun's free hand tightened into a fist as the transfer was made. His normally ruddy color paled. 'Marty?'

Martin's first words were more of a wail. It took a few moments for Aggarun to be able to calm the boy enough for the listening men to make out what he was saying.

'Papa!' Martin sobbed.

Aggarun took charge over the phone, asking questions, demanding that the boy stop his crying and answer intelligently.

'Is the babysitter there?'

'N-no. She called. She's gonna be late.'

'Are you hurt?'

'N-no.'

'Is Barry hurt?'

'N-no.'

Eventually Aggarun extracted the information that the two boys were making their own breakfast.

'But there's only one slice of bread,' Martin wailed.

'Can't you share with your brother?'

'Well, we decided to do Paper, Scissors, Rock and the winner would get the whole piece.'

Aggarun's pallor was growing redder as the story dragged out. 'And?' he urged.

'I won,' the boy sobbed.

'So?' his father demanded.

'It was supposed to be my toast.'

'You won, didn't you? And you're bigger. So what's the problem. I don't see how Barry could take it away from you.'

'He didn't dare. But he got mad. Said I cheated.'

'So?'

'Then he spat on my toast!' the boy wailed.

Aggarun held the phone away from him, glancing helplessly at his staff sitting forward on their chairs.

Dennis was the first to chuckle, then Gene, and then all the rest. They laughed until there were tears in their eyes and Aggarun himself was holding his side.

'It's all right, Marty,' the widower soothed his son. 'This meeting is about over anyway. I'll stop and pick up a loaf of bread - two loaves, one for each of you - on my way home. I'm coming, son. I'm on my way.'

As he set down the receiver, Aggarun wiped his eyes, glanced at his staff and knew without their saying anything how much these men cared about him and his orphaned boys.

'I can't top that one,' he chuckled, shaking his head. 'Meeting's adjourned. Oh, and thank you. Thank you for everything.'

'We'll top the day's record, no matter what it is,' Clint promised.

'I wouldn't doubt it a bit,' Aggarun smiled. 'Nothing would surprise me today.'

He left, striding to the newly traded VW bus.

'He is human,' Clint observed.

'Oh, yeah,' Dennis agreed. 'Nothing like having to raise two small boys on your own to make even the strongest of us human.'

GUMMING IT UP

Angela blinked as she cradled the receiver. 'Not Emma,' she whispered. 'Not our little girl.' Where had they gone wrong?

Shaking her head, Angie washed her hands again at the kitchen sink and returned to chopping the extra celery and onions for the traditional spaghetti sauce her family loved. She still didn't use quite enough oregano, according to her mother-in-law, but even her father-in-law's eyebrows lifted in appreciation of her cooking, so Angie was satisfied to slow-cook the sauce the way Burt and Enid and Emma liked it best.

'Hi, Mom!' Emma stood grinning at the kitchen door. Their independent six-year-old with the freckles and sandy brown hair just as unruly as her father's, flipped off her shoes into the corner of the porch. She ran in scarlet socks bedecked with tiny bug-like girls with huge eyes. Angie could never remember their names, only that they were cartoon heroines. 'Whatcha makin'?' Emma asked, her turned up nose snuffing. 'Bisketty?'

That was the family joke, and the nearest little Enid could get to pronouncing their favorite meal. Angie opened her mouth to say something, and then closed it and merely nodded. Wait until Burt came home. Somehow they had to make this an opportunity to teach, not something either one of them should simply react to. Angie looked into Emma's innocent hazel eyes.

'Daddy called. He'll be home in about forty-five minutes, so please get the table set right away.'

'Okay,' Emma agreed. She so much preferred setting the table to helping clear it and washing the dishes. Both Angie and Burt felt it was important for the girls to be given meaningful chores in order to learn to take responsibility. Angie sighed. How could she tell Burt what had happened at Marmon's Foods?

There wasn't time to tell him before supper. Burt came home a few minutes later than he'd hoped and he'd simply sat down at the table so their meal wouldn't be spoiled by waiting for him to shower.

'It's relaxing, Angie, not a necessity,' he laughed, then quickly lifted his arm to sniff. 'Or is it?'

'No, no, you're fine,' she giggled, loving the way he seldom took himself seriously. Pompous, he wasn't. 'Come on, then. Spaghetti's on!'

At the table, he made them laugh with his tales about the characters and adventures around the airport. The little girls beamed at their father. They adored him, and they knew the feelings were mutual. There was nothing more important in Burt's life than his family. For a moment, Angie was tempted not to even tell him. But that wasn't fair. They'd always discussed everything, even the things that hurt to know.

'Honey,' Angie said when the little girls had scooted off to the family room to play dolls and watch the video of those bug-eyed cartoons. Burt was standing up, stretching, ready to go for his shower. As he saw her face, he sat back down.

'What is it?'

'No, nothing dire. We're okay. It's just that the girls and I went to Marmons' this afternoon. They've got the best produce. I think I'd go to them even if they weren't so near.'

'You love shopping at a Mom and Pop store,' he nodded, his eyes narrowing.

'Yes, I love knowing the people so well.'

'But what about their also knowing us so well?' He was quick to follow. That made it easier.

'Yes, well, I did get a call just before you came home.'

'From Marmons? And?'

'Mrs. Marmon sounded like she hated to tell me, but her son, you know, the middle one - Larry, isn't it? - he's home for a break from college and helping out for a couple days. He saw Emma taking a package of chewing gum. And then he saw her put it in her pocket. He didn't want to make a fuss. But Mrs. Marmon said she knew how we'd tried to teach the girls honesty, and she felt we'd want to know. She wasn't mad or anything. She just felt we'd like to know.'

'What a kind woman,' Burt said, but his brown eyes had narrowed in pain for the little girl he loved. 'We're going to have to...'

'Dad?' Emma called from the doorway.

Both the parents startled and looked at each other. How long at Em been there? How much had she heard? Evidently nothing much from the innocent way she approached them.

'Yes, daughter?' Burt answered, reaching out for her.

She rushed to him and he picked her up onto his lap. They were instantly into a gentle bantering that left Angie smiling as she moved away to gather the dirty dishes. She was carrying the stack toward the kitchen when Burt coughed. Angie turned back to look. It sounded deep and serious.

45

Emma stood at his knee where he'd hurriedly set her down from his lap. Her mouth was opened in an 'O' and her dark eyes narrowed with concern.

'Burt?' Angie called low, stepping back to set the plates back on the table. But he caught her eye and she knew he'd figured out at gentle way to deal with the stealing episode. She nodded and walked again toward the kitchen, stopping just inside the door where she could listen.

'Oh, if only I had a piece of gum,' Burt managed between coughs. 'It would probably soothe my throat.'

'I've got gum, Daddy,' Emma cried. She dashed away.

Angie set the dishes in the sink and came back to the doorway to watch as Emma returned, dragging the jacket she'd worn that afternoon to the market.

'Here, Daddy, here's gum for you!' She thrust the unopened packet into her father's hands, smiling and pleased to be able to help.

Mother and daughter watched as Burt meticulously opened the wrapper and wedged out a stick of gum. He slid off the paper sleeve and unwrapped the foil. He looked at the pink stick a moment before rolling it and putting it into his mouth.

For a moment he relaxed as though his throat were in fact eased. Emma nearly clapped her hands in delight, but stopped when Burt's forehead wrinkled and his cheeks and mouth twisted.

'Daddy, what? Does it taste bad?'

Burt sat up, considering. 'This... ' He chewed again, tentatively. 'This tastes like STOLEN gum,' he said.

Emma's mouth gaped open as she lifted her face to stare at her father. Her dark eyes widened and then her face paled. She looked as though she would break into tears. Slowly she lowered her eyes, and then her head.

'Oh,' she whispered.

HOSANNA!

Four-year-old Logan's eyes sparkled as he waved his palm branch. "Mom!" he cried, "It was so cool! We marched into the church and everybody was watching us coming and waving these palms all over the place and we were hollering, 'Hosanna! Hosanna!'"

"That's what Palm Sunday is all about, Logan. People are even happier now two thousand years later because we finally realize what an enormous gift we've received."

"Gee, Mom, who is this Hosanna guy then? Is he the Santa that lives at the South Pole?"

BRIAN'S INSIGHT

'Didn't you hate them, Grandma?' Brian looked up with those wide, dark eyes that saw so much for a seven-year-old.

'Hate?' Peggy let her shoulders sag forward just a bit from their accustomed straight line. Finally she shook her head and gazed at the boy. 'We Dutch are a people taught from childhood to be gentle and courteous. I've often thought those traits give you time to consider what is really going on before you've let your own reactions take over.'

It was Brian's turn to shake his head.

'Anger and revenge and retaliation and hate - I think those are consuming emotional habits that will take over your life, if you let them, Brian. And they are habits. Each time we let them take over, it is more difficult the next time a situation arises not to allow them to take over again. They destroy. They destroy what you hate.

They destroy even more quickly the best that is inside you.'

'You learned that in the Japanese concentration camp?'

'Perhaps it was the wisdom of my early life in Holland fortifying me to face what came when I was a young girl in Dutch Indonesia,' Peg said, her hands smoothing her skirt. Conditions had been so appalling, she wasn't sure she'd have been strong enough to learn the lessons from the ground up in the 1940's.

'Well, you did feel stuff, didn't you?'

'You mean, did I have moments of anger and desires for revenge? Yes, of course, the emotions played over me.'

'Well, they're sure playing over me now,' the child said. 'Larry is sure making me mad.'

'Are you going to give Larry power over you to "make" you anything?'

Brian did a quarter-turn away from her. The flush of peevishness was one he hadn't felt often and it had a strangely enticing grip on him, stirring parts of himself he'd only been vaguely aware of before.

'Every person has...' Peggy began.

'I know, I know,' he interrupted and then was instantly contrite at her expression. He lowered his eyes a moment, then met hers. She'd been too close and too loving and comforting all his young life for him to deliberately hurt her now. He smiled. 'Each person has a gift,' he said, quoting her wisdom. 'Each of us has something unique and priceless about us that is only and completely our own.'

'It isn't always easy to find,' Peggy nodded.

'It sure isn't,' Brian agreed. 'Especially in Larry. But I'll find it,' he said, lifting his frail shoulders in determination.

It wasn't, but he did.

He watched Larry. He studied Larry with forehead contracted in concentration. He watched Larry from the moment the larger boy alighted from his bicycle in the schoolyard in the morning, through every interaction with every first and second-grader and teacher throughout the day. Brian stood watching Larry saunter to the bike rack to go home in the afternoon. Brian even contrived to be two people behind Larry in the lunch line so he could watch how Larry treated the cafeteria workers.

After two days of this scrutiny, Larry did what everyone who saw what was going on expected that Larry would do. During recess, Larry strode up to Brian and stood, feet apart, towering over the little scholar.

'Aw right, squeak, what's goin' on? Why are you staring at me like I'm some new beetle for your bug collection?'

Brian lifted his eyes from Larry's shirt button to peer into the bigger boy's face. 'I'm trying to see what your talent is.'

'What?' Larry frowned.

'My Peggy says everybody's got a talent, something that makes that person unique and valuable, but I told her you didn't. You were just a bully.'

'Whoa,' Larry said, low and menacingly.

'But my Peggy said no, everybody's got a talent and I just had to look and look and I'd find yours. So I'm looking.'

A few of the second graders who'd gathered around them started tittering. Gene, no friend of Larry or of Brian, hurled a taunt that set them laughing louder. 'You'll need binoculars, Brian. Maybe even a microscope.'

'The squeak's probably got both at home,' called another who was piqued by Brian's advanced knowledge of science as well as everything else.

That set the entire group free to jibe and poke insults.

'Hey, leave him alone,' Larry warned when one of the bigger boys started to push Brian from behind. 'He's mine,' Larry added, but that hadn't been what prompted his initial protest, Brian knew.

At that moment Miss Pearman's no-nonsense voice told them, 'Break it up!'

The children at the edges sidled away. The ones caught in Miss Pearman's fierce gaze, stood head-down as she worked her way to the center of the circle.

'All right, what is happening here? Who started this?'

All eyes down, the children nevertheless could see Larry shift his weight and lift his face to the teacher.

'Nothing, Miss Pearman. It wasn't nothing. I asked Brian here about a beetle and he was trying to tell me what made it tick and everybody come over to see, too. That's all.'

Brian caught a flicker of amusement twitch at the young teacher's lips. She had seen Brian tagging along behind Larry these last few days and she knew as well as the others that Larry, being Larry, wouldn't stand for that forever. But it was Larry himself who was giving her this friend-saving excuse, and Miss Pearman loved children enough to be willing to accept it as long as no harm had been done. She studied Brian for marks of a scuffle. And then, belatedly, she examined Larry. No harm, no foul, she reasoned.

'Recess is nearly over. You children start heading back toward the school,' she said firmly.

They scattered, exhaling as though released from danger. But Larry and Brian she caught by the shoulders.

'And just where is this beetle you found, Larry? I'd like to see it myself.'

'Ahh-h...' Larry stammered.

'We let it go, Miss Pearman,' Brian said straight-faced. 'It was something between us and we let it go.'

'I see,' she nodded. 'All right, then, I'm letting you two go. But just remember I'll be watching. There won't be any fighting, you hear me?'

'No fighting,' Brian promised solemnly.

Larry looked as though he'd been stripped of his weapons as he entered a bear pit, but at Miss Pearman's insistent look, he finally nodded.

'Say it, Larry.'

'No fighting, Miss Pearman,' he stammered, curling his lip at Brian.

Throughout the rest of the day, Larry caught Brian peering at him only twice more. The second time, Brian's dark eyes lighted up in understanding. Larry stared at him a moment and was met with such a wide grin of fellowship, that it was Larry who looked away, puzzled and strangely moved.

Brian seemed distracted the rest of the day, which was quite unlike him. But Miss Pearman had told his teacher about the incident in the schoolyard and she decided simply to keep an eye on the boys for another day or so.

As soon as school was out, Larry took off for the bike racks. Brian gathered his books and took off after him. He had to half-run to catch up with Larry's longer strides, but Brian was excited to tell his new friend what he'd discovered.

'He is my friend, Peggy!' Brian told her that afternoon when she picked him up.

Peggy smiled at her grandson's radiance. She knew how hard he'd worked on that self-appointed task. She nodded. 'I'm glad,' she said.

'I told him that I studied three days to find his talent until I finally did.'

'Did you tell him what it was?'

'I told him he seemed like a bully and so negative about everything, but then I realized that IS his talent: to question everything and to never take anybody's word about anything. And it is a talent, Peggy, to be a questioner like that. It takes courage to always make sure you find out things for yourself. But it sure makes people uncomfortable with you sometimes.'

Peggy glanced over at this small boy with the enormous ability to see below the surface to what was real underneath.

'Did you tell him that, Brian?'

'Oh, yes. And he looked shocked. I don't think anybody had ever told him he was courageous before.' Brian smiled happily and Peggy breathed out slowly, careful to mask her tremendous pride in the child. It was his moment, and her feelings must not get in the way of his discoveries. She caught only a glimpse of Brian's frown and turned quickly to look at him before again facing the road. What could be wrong? She didn't have long to wait to find out and it wasn't at all what she'd been expecting.

'I wonder, Peggy, do you think we could find a way for Larry to still question but to do it so he doesn't hurt so many people's feelings?'

She nodded, swallowing to keep from reaching to draw him to her on the front seat. Such insight must not be spoiled by tying it to the reactions of another person. It was his and he deserved to evaluate it on his own. She could tell him later how proud she was of him. For now, she merely smiled.

'I wouldn't be surprised that the two of you could work on that together. Deep friendships can be built on such discoveries, Brian.'

'Yes,' he said, frowning again. 'But even if we don't get to be lifelong buddies, Peggy, I think it would help us both to learn how to do something like that. Not everybody likes me either, you know.'

'Oh?' Peggy murmured. It was difficult for her to believe that not everyone would adore this brilliant little boy. 'I do, you know.'

'Oh, yes, I know!' Brian laughed. 'But you're supposed to. It's your job. You're my grandma.'

LADDER UPWARDS

Most of the boys in Shop Class opted to make napkin holders or cutting boards shaped like pigs. But one, a born instigator, took the time to ask his father what he would like.

'Got enough cutting boards, I reckon, Ed,' Mr. Ortman said. 'And napkin holders. And never did see much use for them napkin rings. What I really need around the place is a good, solid ladder.'

Mr. W's eyes narrowed as he looked at Ed. 'A ladder?' He squinted, wondering for that moment whether this imp was putting him on. But for once the boy seemed genuine. Of course, he'd had years of practice holding that straight face. Mr. W knew of a number of teachers who had taken him at his word and made themselves the brunt of his jokes. Still, (Mr. W shifted his wiry weight from one foot to the other), if the kid was truly interested in making a ladder for his father, then there was no way the teacher wanted to break his spirit of innovation and curiosity. There is nothing more rewarding for a young person that actually bringing to fruition a difficult project. That sense of triumph could be there as a foundation no one could take away from him for the rest of his life.

Mr. W, Loyd Wells, had grown up fighting the Oklahoma droughts and the devastation to a man's pocketbook and soul by the Great Depression. He'd had to leave his young bride with their firstborn when he went into service in World War II. Loyd knew what it was to fight. And maybe it was time that this boy learned, too.

'Well,' Mr. W answered slowly, 'I don't think anybody in my class has ever made a ladder before. If that's what you want, you'll have to do the research and find a plan we can work from.'

Ed's eyes opened and his surly mouth relaxed into a grin. 'You mean I can make my dad a ladder like he wants?'

Mr. W nodded, still not sure about this boy. 'If you work up a feasible plan, yes.'

There, the ball was back in Ed's court. Mr. W had to admit there was a moment there when part of him would have said Ed deserved it if he didn't make that ladder. He'd been a pain in one neck after the other among the school faculty.

But that twinge was only momentary. There was something in the boy's green eyes. Something hopeful instead of sneering. Some spark that said to the teacher's soul, we may win this one, Ed and I.

Behind his back, Mr. W crossed his fingers and murmured a little prayer while he nodded and suggested and frowned and otherwise responded to the boy's ideas.

Of course the first plan was so elaborate and so intricately sketched that Loyd himself would have had to concentrate to build it. And the second and the third looked great but wouldn't be practical. With the fancy dowels and hinges, they were more for decoration than for heavy use. And Ed's dad wanted a ladder that would last him for years of daily moving and treading and leaning and hauling and climbing to the top, despite the warnings against overbalancing. Every man took a chance or two with his ladder when it looked as though it would save him work. Whatever Ed's sense of accomplishment for having built that ladder, it would be lost if his father were ever hurt because of it.

Several times the boy's expression told of his frustration, and then even a sense of betrayal. Ed clearly thought his teacher was putting him off, turning down plan after plan, picture after picture, for reasons of his own. Maybe the shop teacher wasn't so great with wood after all and couldn't really do the project.

But that couldn't be the reason. For one thing, he'd watched Mr. W handle mistakes his students made. With a clever twist or planing, he'd take a surefire loss and make it into something worthwhile. Ed knew that Mr. W was a magician with wood. Ed had seen the magic.

And then he thought Mr. W had it in for Ed himself. He'd pulled a couple stunts those first days of high school last fall. Not all of the laughter he'd egged on had been with, instead of at Mr. W, and the teacher must have known.

But Ed wanted to make that ladder and he knew Mr. W would help him if he could find the right one to make.

Reluctantly, Ed started doing hard research. He looked carefully at the drawings and the pictures of finished ladders to see what Mr. W could possibly object to. And then he found exactly the right one - angles right, no fancywork, reinforcement where it was needed. Perfect!

Ed had quite a time screwing on a nonchalant expression when he took the plan for Mr. W's approval. He couldn't keep a certain sparkle out of his eyes or a grin from sliding onto his lips as he watched the teacher assess each feature carefully. And then he felt his lips tighten. Mr. W was scowling. He'd found a flaw. Ed could feel the anger and frustration rising from the pit of his stomach. He pressed his lips and clenched his hands to keep from snapping something that would end the project for sure. And the end would be his fault, not this snooty shop teacher's. He'd have won.

Mr. W didn't look up. At least not that Ed could see. But the boy's tension was palpable.

Mr. W was tempted for that moment to accept the plan. It was a fine ladder, after all. And it would probably do nicely. But...

'The only thing I have a problem with on this one is the stance. See how narrow the upper angle is?'

Ed glared. But Mr. W was right. If Dad stepped on the rungs above the pail tray, the whole ladder could wobble. Ed had learned that much assessing plan after rejected plan. His head jerked in a nod he'd rather not have let Mr. W see.

'But if we...'

Ed couldn't believe his ears. But he could believe his eyes. Mr. W was using his pencil to shave a little here and enlarge a pin or hinge there.

'That could work,' Ed said, knowing that it could. His finger darted forward, pointing at the angle of the feet. 'We'll have to alter the angle there, too, or it won't sit flat once we change that hinge.'

Mr. W was looking at him as one carpenter to another. 'You'll have to do that, too,' he agreed.

'You,' not 'We.' This was Ed's project. And Mr. W promised in that look to be at his shoulder watching out for the best outcome. But the ladder, like the plan, would be Ed's responsibility.

Ed stood a little taller, nodding without the sneer that usually took so much work to maintain. He had other places for that energy to go now.

'I'll redraw this with all the new angles figured and let you take a look before I get the materials lined up.'

Mr. W just nodded. No 'I told you so.' No plastic words of assurance or congratulations. Just a nod.

Ed brought his young son to Mr. W's Celebration of Life. He stood and told the story of the ladder, and the multiple projects that followed as Ed took as many shop classes from his mentor as he could jam into his schedule.

He stood with tears glistening as he told the gathered family and friends how Mr. W had guided him from behind.

'I truly believe that Mr. Wells was the first teacher who took any interest in who I really was and not the snotty little brat that most teachers saw. I've now spent over twenty years in the wood products industry. I'm the general manager of a Kitchen and Bath manufacturer. And I still have all my fingers,' Ed smiled and raised both hands for everyone to count ten.

'Best of all, my dad still has that ladder leaning against his house for everyday use.' Ed drew back his shoulders. 'Thanks, Mr. W.'

ANGRY TEEN ANGEL

'The ugly duckling, that's what I am,' Karen hissed at the mirror.

Chris peered over at her twin. 'What?'

Although they were identical, there was no way Chris was an ugly duckling. Karen shook her head murmuring, 'Nothing. It's just - it's just that..."

'Ron didn't pay much attention to you at Youth group tonight? Oh, Karen, he's so much older. Why would he be bothered with either one of us, or anybody our age? We must seem like babies to him. And you're not ugly. If you are, then I am, too. And I don't feel ugly.' She tossed her long, striking blond hair over her shoulder and treated her sister to one of her dazzling smiles, even batting her eyelashes. At Karen's expression, she grinned and tossed a pillow across the bed. "You're beautiful, if I do say so myself,' she laughed.

In a way, it was true. Plumping the pillow and laying it at the head of her bed, Karen turned back to pose in front of the mirror.

It was true. They were beautiful, or at least they were getting there. Their legginess and awkwardness were being replaced by curve and grace so gradually you didn't notice it from one day to the next. But over time, you realized they were becoming fascinating, attractive young women. The stringy hair now glowed under the hundred brush-strokes each night. It caught the light and shone around Karen's oval face. The eyes were startlingly blue, and Chris was teaching her to use eyeliner to make them stand out. Chris was learning a lot from her fellow cheerleaders. And there was a lot to learn. But you had to be fiercely competitive to try to join that squad, and Karen wasn't. She preferred to have Chris learn the tricks and bring them home to share with her older-by-minutes sister. Besides...

Chris questioned with her neatly arched eyebrows whether it was time to switch off the princess lamp between their beds. Besides, Karen nodded, lost in realizing that she simply didn't have the energy to keep up with those cheerleaders any more.

'Okay,' Karen agreed aloud. Chris turned off the light, leaving their room on the second floor of the rambling old house suffused with light filtered through the aged trees from the street lamp on the corner of Elm Street.

'Good night, Beautiful,' Chris whispered. 'God bless.'

'Go with God,' Karen whispered back and turned her back on her sister. They'd said their prayers together since they could babble, "mama." But in these last few weeks and months, they'd grown apart. Karen could feel it. Or not exactly grown apart so much as Chris continuing on their merry way while Karen could barely stand up, let alone stagger in pursuit.

The trouble was, Ron was so darned cute. Dad had known his family for years and liked them a lot. Ron came to Youth at the church. He had a grin that made the twins' eyes pop. He was pretty tall and broad shouldered. He was older, just enough to make him exciting. Who wouldn't go ga-ga over a college man? Warner Pacific College. He was actually going to college in Portland and here were the twins mere Juniors in high school.

Karen sighed and climbed into bed, weak and tired. It made her so mad to be this tired. She hadn't really done anything.

'It's all that weight you've been losing,' Mama griped the next morning at breakfast. 'I don't understand how you girls want to ruin your health just to be pretty in someone else's eyes.'

But even Mama lately was watching closely and realizing that Karen did eat. Not a lot at a time, but often. So often. She was sometimes ravenously hungry only a couple hours after the last time she'd had a meal.

And drinking water. My goodness, how she chugged down water. She knew every fountain and girls' room in the high school and was a frequent visitor to both. In fact, sometimes she was in agony before her class was finished. She stuffed extra clothes in her locker, just in case there was a long line at the bathroom. And she always sat at the end of the row at the movies or the Friday night football games.

It was so annoying. Chris didn't have to worry and run like that. Run, she did, but not just to make it to the ladies room in time to keep from humiliating herself. She waved at Karen and gave Mama one of those flying kisses on the cheek she was famous for as she fled the kitchen.

'I'll be late for special practice for the squad,' she called back over her shoulder.

Karen could hear their brother Bill toot to say he had his car warmed up and ready to take her to high school. But Karen didn't feel so good this morning. As much as she'd like a ride with Bill and Chris, she just wasn't up to scurrying. She lifted one hand to wave out the window to go on without her.

Karen picked up her spoon and traced the patterns made by faint shadows of leaves projected onto the round oak tabletop.

Chris was gorgeous and vital. Sometimes when they sang duets for Dad's church or the state Church of God conventions, Karen felt like an echo of her vibrant sister. Even her voice wasn't as strong and full of color as it always had been. She could still create songs and arrangements for them to sing, just as Chris did, but her voice lately was sounding as tired as Karen herself felt.

'It isn't my imagination, either,' Karen whispered grimly to her spoon. 'I couldn't," she muttered again and again, squeezing her eyes tight shut to close off the tears.

She used to come up behind Ron and leap onto his back for a piggyback ride. Sometimes she could completely surprise him, though he always knew who it was. He had such a throaty laugh when she clambered up without his having been aware she was near enough to attack him.

She'd come up while he was talking with Chris and a couple of the others last night at Youth. But she couldn't make the jump up onto his back. She just physically couldn't leap that high. It scared her.

Chris had recognized what she was about to do and made some comment about how much more grown-up it was not to jump up that childish way any more. But it hadn't been sophistication but fatigue that had stopped her last night. Karen loved being on Ron's back, or holding him close in front, as if that were acceptable.

Mama would have a fit if she knew about Karen's dreams. Poor Mama, if she only knew. Poor me, Karen smiled at her distorted reflection in the bowl of the spoon. Poor me, if Mama even suspected.

David came in with Tim and Charlie in tow, stuffed a piece of toast into their hands and nodded to Mama. 'I'll get them to school on time,' he called as he herded the littlest brothers out onto the enclosed back porch and down the wood steps.

It was a hassle getting nine of them off in the morning. They were all within walking distance, but it was an unusual morning when all nine were ready and out the door in time to walk. Dad was already off paying a pastoral call or opening up his carpentry shop or galloping to the fire station where he volunteered - in his spare time. But Karen hadn't heard a siren or the phone ring. Either of those sounds was so common in their house that she could easily have ignored it, not even really hearing it, though her hearing was exceptional.

'I'm glad something about me is exceptional,' she whispered to the spoon, not believing a complementary word.

Mama came back and stood at the doorway peering at Karen's back. After a minute, she sighed and sat down at the table one over from directly beside her first daughter. Seven sons and twin daughters. How she loved them all, and ached for each one when something was wrong. And there was clearly something terribly wrong now with Karen. She just hoped it didn't have anything to do with young Ron. But she didn't think it did.

'Sugar Girl,' she said softly and laid her worn hand on the table between them. 'What's wrong? Not feeling well this morning?'

The doctor looked between anxious mother and wide-eyed, terrified daughter. 'Diabetes,' he said. His diagnosis sounded so heavy, like a tolling of a somber bell, and indeed, it was. Diabetes mellitus could be such an unfair disease, making dire changes in nearly every system of the body. 'My nurse is making arrangements to put Karen into the hospital now. We're going to have to get that blood sugar under control. It's sky-high. And I'll bet there are times when you've nearly fainted, aren't there, young lady?"

Karen, white-faced, nodded. Oh, how many times. 'Diabetes?' she asked. 'Then, it's something you can control?'

'I hope so,' he answered fervently. But he didn't have much hope.

Karen's blood sugars were all over the place. She hated the idea of giving herself insulin shots. She hated being different, of somehow being less than the other kids. Before, when she was pretty and singing beside her glamorous twin, she'd felt special sometimes. People were looking and liking and envying. Now they saw her as defective. It wasn't fair.

As much as she was physically able, Karen kept up with her classmates. One class she did enjoy was Office Simulation Lab. They were learning how to handle themselves in an office situation. They even got to go on a field trip to Portland to see various offices first hand. The trip was great. Karen knew she could work in these settings and do herself proud. She was pretty excited as the group sat together at one table in the restaurant afterwards. The chaperones sat at another.

As they compared notes and gossip, the young people realized that Liza, one of the chaperones, had ordered a glass of wine with her meal.

Karen blinked. Her pastor father and church-building mother would definitely not have approved of that, especially when she was responsible for a whole gaggle of teenagers. But Liza was the adult, and it wasn't up to Karen to say anything, no matter how she felt. Karen stared at her own meal and began eating, chewing slowly.

Her plate wasn't that different from everyone else's and she'd been really careful the last several days so she'd have extra allowances for treats. The last thing in the world she wanted was to have her friends know how restricted she was. She didn't want them to see her digging needles into herself. She didn't want them to know how the diabetes had taken over her life. She wanted to be a normal high school kid with energy and vibrancy and vitality.

The waitress came to clear most of the dishes. Karen was one of the slowest, so when the ice cream was passed out to everyone, she was nearly the last to receive hers.

Karen grinned up as the waitress slipped the short-stemmed clear glass on the tiny white plate on the placemat in front of her. The scoop of Neapolitan had almost no chocolate, but lots of strawberry, just the way Karen had always liked it.

Karen lifted her spoon and made a joke, tickling her friends. They were laughing together when Liza, Karen could see from the corner of her eye, rose from her table and came walking over to theirs.

Karen paused with the spoon of ice cream at her lips. She'd gone cold, knowing somehow that her worst nightmare was about to come true and there wasn't anything she could do to stop it. Nothing that Dad or Mama would allow, at any rate.

It was so unfair. She hadn't said anything about disapproving of Liza's drinking that glass of wine in front of all of them. But here she was, coming over to their table to say something to Karen in front of all her friends. Slowly, Karen lowered her spoon and set it at the edge of the little white plate.

Liza didn't say anything. For a moment, Karen was hoping whatever had brought Liza to their table, it wasn't going to humiliate Karen. She glanced up, trying to smile at Liza, but the woman's face, slightly flushed, was firm.

Liza said nothing, but she did reach over Karen's shoulder and physically pick up the dish of ice cream and take it away. Karen could see without moving her head that Liza carried it to the chaperone's table and set it there beside her coffee cup. Karen snuck a peek from her lowered eyes. Her friends sat stunned and embarrassed. No one said a word until her best friend sat back, setting down her spoon with a clatter. She pushed back in her chair.

'No,' Karen whispered fiercely, 'don't say anything, Annie.'

Instead, Karen got up and walked as slowly as she could manage to the Ladies' Room. She could feel hot tears welling, but she would not for all her family pride let anyone see those burning tears of humiliation.

Almost three decades later, Karen lifts her shoulders and breathes out, nostrils flaring, as she remembers bawling in that Ladies' Room. She remembers Mama taking her to see a faith healer, and when that didn't work, she remembers feeling that she was letting everyone down. She remembers the devastation of realizing that the God she had prayed to and her family had devoted their whole beings to all of their lives - God would not heal her.

It began the closet eating, so no one would know. If they didn't know, they couldn't disapprove.

It was twenty years and a vicious automobile accident later before Karen came to terms with her diabetes. She shakes her head now, wishing there were a way to reach teenagers with Diabetes, a way to tell them that the discipline is not only worth it, it is vital for any health at all. She tries. She teaches. She sings, she lives a life of loving and sharing through her church and her family.

What a terrible burden for young shoulders. And how difficult it is for those of us who see only from the outside to be there for a juvenile fighting not only growing up but also a disease that takes over her very life and health. But Karen knows, from deep inside. And that knowledge makes her effective as a teacher, a confidant, an encourager. "No matter how unfair it is, diabetes doesn't have to take your whole life," she says, and the kids know she knows what she's talking about.

NIGHT BAG

When darkness covers rural Maine, the stars hurl their light. The moon reigns in pale triumph. But hundred foot trees pierce the silver cover, rendering the earth dark in a way no city dweller can imagine blackness except in the instant before unconsciousness.

At night, rural Mainiacs are akin to Russian peasants in their bone-knowledge of evil forces roaming the earth in search of solitary prey.

Larry parked the ice cream truck and locked the freezers and then the truck door he'd kept open all day to eager-faced youngsters clutching their dimes and quarters. He'd worked until sunset and into the dusk that settles like a haze over the riverport. His jangling bell sound still ringing in his ears, he gathered the two quarts of blackberry' swirl ice cream he'd promised Ma and started across the dairy parking lot. All the milk delivery trucks were lined up. Larry counted them as he crunched past on the gravel. Even his father's battered commercial delivery van stood where he'd left it slightly out of line with the others. Larry was the last done again today.

Larry still had to cross the highway - there'd be little or no traffic on Route 1 this time of night - and hike the one and three-quarters miles up their side road to his father's home where his stepmother may or may not have saved him dinner. That depended on how much the passel of half-sisters and brothers liked what she'd cooked.

Larry sighed over the growling of his stomach. He had never particularly liked ice cream. Though he'd scooped its various colors and textures for kiddies every day this sultry summer, he seldom indulged himself with it. He needed the profits if he was going to make up the difference between what the scholarships covered and what the university charged.

A lone pair of headlights shown coming up from the south, and then were hidden behind a stand of fir as Larry crossed Route 1. He thought of the story his dad told of the trucker just up the road from the dairy who'd backed his flatbed across the road years ago. He was only repositioning it on his mud lawn so visitors could get their car out, so he didn't bother switching on the lights. The car that hit him left no skid marks. The flatbed was skewed a little out of alignment. The car - and the driver- were decapitated. In the dark, the guy'd had no clue.

And that was on the highway, with open spaces on either side at times.

On Shanken Road the old trees grew tall on both sides. Tall, meaning eighty, a hundred plus towering feet. And dense. They grew to within six feet of the sides of the road only paved for the first time just after Julius was born. Warmth still radiated up from the macadam, though already the air kept shaded through most of the day by the trees was turning cool. But it was firm under Larry's size thirteen shoes as he strode. He shifted the short stack of ice cream cartons to his right arm. They were cold.

The moon gleamed on the straight, two-lane road, making it look like liquid mercury shimmering ahead. That was eerie enough, but when the moon shifted from directly overhead, Larry knew, there'd be weird shadows roiling at each side of the road as the silver filtered through sighing, shifting branches.

This was just the weird time of night that Larry's father hated most.

Larry chuckled, remembering his father's fear and the lengths he went to to deal with it. Before any of them could drive, before Larry himself was old enough to be left alone with the swarm of little ones, Pa would come home late from his milk route parking his delivery van at the side of Shanken Road beyond the rail fence. He'd scoot across the yard and reach for the car keys from the peg in the wall high inside the front door, wave to his brood and stride on those long, thin legs to the old Chevy. Ma and Larry would block the kids from crowding out beyond the rail. They'd stand watching as Pa fired up the Chevy and backed it onto Shanken Road and pulled forward about fifty feet up the road past the van and park at the side. He'd open that screeching, rusty Chevy door and haul his long body out and walk back to the van, rev up its engine and pull forward toward Highway 1. The kids watched open-mouthed every time as Pa drove the van fifty feet up the road past the Chevy and pulled to the side and stride back to open that squealing door. They watched until the trees hid Pa's leap frogging the Chevy and van fifty feet at a time. They knew it would be a while before he drove the Chevy home from the dairy, where'd he'd finally parked the van for the final time that night.

At the time, those summers when Larry was still small, Pa's hatred of walking back in the dark had seemed funny. Right now, as Larry walked alone, listening to the whir of wings as a large bird shifted position in the trees above and behind him, the idea of a ride home didn't seem silly at all. In fact, it not only made sense, it gave Larry a reason to admire his father's ingenuity.

A skittering in the brush immediately beside him made Larry jump. When he'd swallowed and could breathe easily again, he noticed a paper bag discarded in the ditch.

The blackberry swirl ice cream was so cold on his arm that he'd shifted it a dozen times already and he was only half way home.

'Well, maybe,' he thought. And being an athletic young man just out of high school, he leaped into the ditch, snatched up the bag and dropped the cartons inside. It was a whole lot easier carrying the frozen treats suspended in the paper.

With renewed nonchalance, Larry loped the rest of the way and vaulted the rail fence as a shortcut across the yard to the front door.

Ma had saved him a little of the stew. 'But only because I didn't put the whole pot on the table, Larry. Them kids gobbled up theirs so you just be glad I saved some for you,' she said.

He was. After a thirteen-hour day selling and the brisk walk home, his gut growled aloud in anticipation.

'And you'll be glad, too, Ma,' he said, tossing the paper bag onto the Formica table as he headed for the wash basin. 'Blackberry swirl. I saved you the last two.'

'Oh yeah?' Ma wide face broke into a smile over her several chins. 'Blackberry', huh?'

'Ma?' Julius's voice squeaked. It had been doing that a lot lately. 'Hey, Larry,' he said, and Larry looked over. The voice was not just that of a fourteen-year-old moving awkwardly into puberty. There was fear there.

'It's okay, Julie,' Larry said low, moving between the boy and the table where the bag was moving on its own.

Ma was already backed against the front door, whimpering and waving the ladle in vaguely threatening patterns. The little kids scampered, squealing toward the living room where Pa, feet up on the coffee table, sat still holding his newspaper, but bending at the waist to peer around the corner into the kitchen.

'It's some sort of trick, huh, Larry?' Julius managed. 'You just said it was ice cream.' His grin was distorted but he could legitimately claim later that he hadn't been fooled one bit, if this was another one of his big brother's gags.

'Don't I wish,' Larry muttered. There was something in that bag, something alive that had already claimed its shelter before Larry had picked it up. Whatever it was, how big could it be since he hadn't felt the extra weight at all? Or at least he hadn't registered the extra weight. But evidently he'd just discounted it as the difference of holding the ice cream suspended rather than on his arm. Oh, boy. Up in these Maine woods, it could be just about anything.

'Where'd you get that there bag, Larry?' Julius's oldest sister Bonnie asked from the living room where two of the smallest kids clung to her.

'I bet it's a skunk,' Agnes said disgustedly from behind Bonnie. 'That'd be just Larry's doing, all right.'

'Whatever it is, get it out of here!' Ma shrilled. But she wasn't moving away from the single door, and that was only way out of the little house.

'Open the screen there in the corner window, Julie,' Larry ordered low.

'Me?' Julius's brown eyes were wide. 'Oh, yeah, okay. I guess so.' To his credit, he moved toward the corner between the Ma at the door and the Formica table where the bag was twisting and bulging.

Larry glanced back at the living room. Pa had moved, but only to draw up his legs and sit higher in the couch. There wasn't a van or a Chevy for Pa to hide in, but Larry was on his own.

Grabbing up the wicker basket beside the basin stand, Larry dumped the trash and peels onto the counter. What he wanted was a shotgun. Wouldn't that bag explode into blood and guts and blackberry spatter if he had a load of buckshot handy? He'd be a week cleaning up the walls and ceiling, but, oh, it would be worth it. Larry felt his trigger finger closing slowly, squeezing the wicker rim.

The bag erupted, but through no fault of Larry's. The movements inside the bag had been growing more frantic, and then the top two-thirds bent and a long, sinuous line of fur emerged. Two small eyes glinted in the light of the electric bulb hanging from the middle of ceiling. And then it was moving.

The trouble was, it didn't know where to move to.

'It is a skunk!' Agnes cried bounding up the stairs to the children's attic bedroom.

'It's a weasel,' Larry corrected but that was only a shade more acceptable. Weasels can be vicious like minks when they're cornered. Their bites can not only be nasty, they can bring on some pretty unhealthy diseases. Larry's first impulse was to leap onto the chair and then the Formica table the weasel had just vacated. He tossed the wicker basket to trap it, but missed.

'Get the kids into Ma's bedroom,' Larry shouted. 'Shut the door!'

Bonnie scooped up the two and waddled to the far corner of the living room, but Pa was there ahead of her and slammed the door in her face. With a grunt, she hustled with her load up the stairs.

'Get something to block the top of the stairs, Agnes,' she yelled. If the weasel started up there, there was nothing to hold it back. Why hadn't Pa waited until the little kids were in his room before he slammed that door?

There wasn't time to worry about that now. Larry trusted Bonnie and Agnes to get something into place although for the life of him - and them - he couldn't think right then of what it could be.

'Throw me the broom, Julie!'

How Julius got to the broom and hurled it across the room before he made it to stand on the table, Larry couldn't fathom. But he was up and relatively safe and Larry now had a weapon, or at least a herder, in his hands.

That left Ma. Deathly pale, with whites showing all the way around the irises the way a horse does in panic, Ma was backed up against the door. The ladle was still waving in the air, now in definitely more threatening but just as useless patterns.

The weasel darted to the nearest dark haven under the counter.

Larry leaped across the room to block the door into the living room. He stood with the broom pointing at the counter floor.

'Ma! Get up on the table with Julius!' Larry yelled, but his stepmother, mouth open, said nothing. She did nothing except gesture with that ladle. 'Ma, move! I'm going to try to sweep him out the door.'

When the long snout peeked at the base of the counter, Larry attacked with the broom, trying to direct the animal back away from the living room and the open staircase where the children cowered.

The weasel ducked and ran. Larry swung at him with the broom. The weasel darted to its right, directly at Ma, who screamed and threw the ladle. It swished by Larry's left ear and clattered into the wall behind him. Larry ducked, belatedly, and lost sight of the weasel. But Ma's scream brought his head up. He just caught sight of her round body bounding toward the living room like an ejected balloon where she collapsed on the floor in a dead faint.

But her choice of direction had convinced the weasel to go the other way. There he was, back in the comparative open space of the kitchen, trembling under the table.

'Julie, grab something and stand at the living room door in front of Ma!' Larry cried.

But Julius was Pa's son, too. He wasn't moving.

In the instant of slow motion Larry reached for the door handle and opened it, wide. Unfortunately, it swung into the kitchen. It wouldn't be a clean sweep from under the table directly to outside. The weasel could well get cornered behind the open door, and there was no telling what it would do when it felt completely trapped.

Larry grasped the broom again with both hands. The weasel slunk down so it was a ribbon of fur and started back for under the counter. Larry was out of position. It could get to the living room with no one to block it. Larry extended that broom and swung, connecting with the animal just before it made it under the counter.

Julius gasped and leaped from the table onto the chair in the far corner as the long fur body hit the edge of the Formica, slithered across and crashed into the wall on the far side.

The weasel lay stunned, but only for a moment. Larry wanted to go straight at it, but the table was in the way. He darted to the left, brushing by Julius, and got to the weasel as it lifted its head, shaking off the effects of its crash into the wall. It saw Larry coming and gathered its legs under it to flee the other way. If it got under the table, it would have clear sailing.

Larry swung that broom like a batter going for a pitch low and so far outside the coach would have his head on a platter for even trying.

But he connected. The weasel lifted into the air. Larry had aimed for the open doorway, but the weasel moved. It was a softball with a corkscrew motion. But there was enough power behind that desperate swing that the animal was lifted and flung - not at the doorway, but out the window. Julius must have loosened that screen. Or Larry had enough adrenaline behind that swing to take the weasel out, screen and all.

Larry stood panting at the window, looking out at the silvery streak of fur taking off across the yard to the woods. Julius stood behind, his eyes nearly as wide as his mother's had been.

'You done it, Larry,' he said. 'He done it!' Julius hollered to give the others the all-clear.

The two young men listened to Agnes and Bonnie on the stairwell. They heard Agnes bending over, assuring Ma groaning as she woke up on the floor. They didn't hear Pa enter until he answered Julius's proud, third, 'He done it!'

'He done it all right,' Pa sneered, blaming Larry for having brought in the weasel in the first place.

Larry turned, ready to snap at Pa for hiding alone and leaving the children to fend for themselves. The words were in his mouth. His fists were clenched tight around that broom handle. He glared at this man and saw his fear naked without the cloak of a child's born admiration for his father. For the first time, Larry saw him man to man, and what he saw made him turn away without answering.

'Sorry,' he managed after a moment. It had been his fault. He should have checked that bag.

Bonnie stood with the two little ones gathered around her at the living room door. She looked at her father and then at her half-brother.

'Anybody for ice cream?' she asked. The children giggled.

Larry peered at her, grateful, and then sad. It would be her burden when he left. And college was only weeks away now.

'Sorry,' he said again. He slipped outside to pick up the screen, but mostly to stand a moment alone, looking at the moon and the stars and the blackness of Maine trees spearing into the night.

ON THE SPOT ●

"'Having three little girls under two years old must have been really something,' people tell me. They always have their eyes and mouths open wide when they say that," Jane adds with a wry smile. "But, honestly, I don't remember it being that bad. Annie was a sweet little girl, and then when the twins came, well, you just cope, that's all. But then," she says with a sigh, "whenever I see pictures that were taken around that time, I do look so tired."

The first couple years were the hardest. Once the little ones were sleeping through most nights, the bags under Jane's eyes gradually faded. But then it was hard to keep up with them all. They were so different. Annie, bright-eyed, tall, inquisitive; Emily, the youngest (by minutes), as gentle-souled as her beautiful great aunt Alfhild; and Amy, the proverbial as well as actual middle child full of spit and vinegar. Amy questioned everyone and everything. Jane welcomed her independence of spirit and mind, but there were times when she would have been grateful for a respite from the little blonde's never-ending queries.

When Jane's sister-in-law brought home a newly adopted daughter, Jane called to ask if it was too soon for the four Hollons to visit.

"No, no, please come!" the sister-in-law answered.

So Jane sat down with the little girls to explain that they were going to see the new baby.

"Your new little cousin is adopted," Jane explained and, remarkably, all three little girls nodded, satisfied with the explanation and eager to see the infant.

They were welcomed at the door and, as each little girl peeled out of her winter coat, she joined in the hush by putting her own chubby finger to her lips.

"Baby's sleeping," they repeated, delighted by the quiet game. Taking Annie's hand in her own, her aunt led the way to the crib so the girls could look in. Jane followed closely with Emily and Amy.

"She's so pretty," whispered Annie, who knew a lot about little babies.

"She's so little," breathed Emily, tossing her long, dark hair.

But Amy reached in and drew back the blanket covering the sleeping baby. Amy frowned and turned to confront her mother.

"She doesn't have spots," Amy declared.

Realizing her little blonde was concerned about something, Jane led the girls gently away to where they could talk.

"What made you think she might have spots, Amy?" Jane asked as the baby's momma closed the door to her room.

"You said."

"I told you she'd have spots?" Jane started. She thought over what she'd explained to the children. "I did tell you that she was adopted."

"Yeah," Amy smiled, repeating exactly what she'd heard: "Polka-dotted."

77

OVERWHELMED

At fifty-five, Gwen was average height and only a little overweight. Her brown hair was trimmed neatly and her make-up, though sparse, was in good taste. But there were dark circles under her hazel eyes, and the crows' feet at the edges were so rigid and so deep that Dr. Holland couldn't imagine her smiling.

She was competent, able, well disciplined. She had worked in the actuarial section of Baseman Insurance for so many years that she'd been thought nearly indispensable. At least she had been until the recent shake-up in the management of the company.

Gwen came to the vision clinic to check out problems with her eyes. 'I've got so much to do at the computer, I simply can't have vision problems,' she told Dr. Holland. 'I can't afford them.'

'You've got a financial drain?' he guessed. 'And an emotional one.'

Gwen stared at him. His empathy was too much; she looked away.

'M-my brother,' she managed finally.

'Health problems?'

'Mentally disabled.'

'Severely?'

'Oh, yes,' she sighed. 'He'll have his fifty-second birthday this month, but he'll enjoy the cake and candles like a four-year-old.'

'Is that the stage of his arrested development? And you've been his caregiver for years? Decades?'

She nodded. 'Oh, I haven't minded. Truly, I haven't. I love him.'

'"He ain't heavy, he's my brother,"' Holland murmured. 'That song must raise bittersweet emotions in you. What kind of help do you have?'

'He goes to a day care center while I'm at work.'

'And that's all?'

'People keep telling me I should put him in a home, but I couldn't do that. Not to James. They don't know him the way I do.

'Besides,' she looked at the floor, 'I can't afford to.'

'Hence the fear of losing your vision - and your income.'

'Fear, yes, but I've got to know. Will you be straight with me and tell me the truth? Am I going blind?'

Holland nodded. 'I did find some problems, especially in your visual fields exam. It shows that you are seeing with your entire retina - that light-sensitive area of the back of your eyeball.'

'But...'

'There are areas on the retina where you are seeing less than you should be.'

'So I'm going blind in those areas?'

'I'm not sure. They may clear up. I'd like to try an experiment and see if we can find out. Is that okay with you?'

'Yes, of course.'

'I'd like you to do a series of tasks while you bounce this ball. When you are mentally organized, you'll be able to read the words on the cards I show you and still keep up the rhythm of your bouncing.'

'Follow the bouncing ball,' she grimaced.

Her unexpected stab at a joke set him laughing. For a moment, she looked at him. But the kindness in his eyes told her that he appreciated her sardonic humor as no one had for a long time. She smiled, pleased. And then she laughed with him.

At the end of the training session, Gwen was more relaxed than she had been in a long time.

'Do you feel up to testing the visual fields again?' Holland asked, and she nodded, but a sudden dread swept over her. What if she really was going blind? What would happen to James? How could she help him if she needed to be led around by the hand herself?

At the completion of the test, Gwen peered at him anxiously until she saw him smile.

'Most of the areas of reduced vision tested before at 20/80 or 20/60. This time they test at 20/30. That a huge improvement, just from your being able to relax and cope.'

'But you weren't sure they would improve?'

'Sometimes the areas of depressed vision are absolute. Whatever cause the block of vision to occur, that blockage has become so imbedded that the perception of light is completely lost.'

'What can cause that kind of block?'

'In our society, it's usually stress. We don't learn how to take a time-out to let ourselves get organized and relax. Prolonged, unrelieved stress causes our senses to constrict down to protect us from overload.'

'So you're telling me my eye problems are all in my head?'

Holland smiled. 'When you're in the middle of a crisis situation, do you hear the birds sing or the patter of raindrops on the roof?'

'You think I'm weak.'

'I think you've been under enormous stress and pain for longer than I can imagine myself holding up under.'

She sat rigid for several minutes, then finally sighed.

'You are a kind man,' she said. 'I asked for you to be straightforward. I don't know how else you could have gotten me to see this for what it is. But I have to admit, the shock therapy wasn't easy to take.'

'You are a woman of courage. I was counting on that.'

'You're telling me that the stress of the world is mine and I can do something about it.'

'It is your world. The choices are yours. But a positive philosophy isn't going to transform your brother into a functional adult.'

'I need realistic choices.'

'And realistic expectations. If your goals are realistic, then you can legitimately achieve them.'

Gwen smiled bitterly. 'That's a degree of wisdom I can't quite take in yet, Dr. Holland.'

'We can only accept when we're ready. Sometimes an effective time-out can be merely a change of subject. It may be helpful to divide the day into segments: morning, afternoon, and evening. Instead of slogging away at something all afternoon, just tell yourself you will put that task on tomorrow morning's agenda when you are fresh. Then do something else. You'll be making progress. You'll feel constructive instead of defeated.'

'If Baseman doesn't keep dinging me to get their agenda done in impossible conditions.'

'One game that works for many of my patients is to visualize somewhere where they've been happy. Close your eyes and picture it in your imagination. Listen, smell. Draw in as many of your sense perceptions as you can. The waves booming on the shore, for instance. Just those few moments can allow your mind to relax and get organized. Whenever you feel yourself getting overwhelmed, take the moment to step away mentally.'

Gwen closed her eyes. 'I do feel better,' she said simply. 'I hope this works at home. And at the insurance company.'

It was more than a year later that Gwen returned to Dr. Holland's clinic. 'How are you?' he asked. Gwen could see that he remembered and he cared.

'I've got good news and bad news.'

'Oh?' He let her choose which to tell him first.

'I'm having trouble with my vision. I'd like to have my eyes tested.'

'Gladly.'

Gwen could tell that the results of the tests were not promising. 'Did those areas of reduced perception clear?'

'I'm afraid not.'

'Oh,' Gwen managed.

'You were afraid of that,' Holland guessed. 'But I have the feeling that was a price you paid.'

'In a way, I guess it was. I'd told you last year about the changes in our company's management?'

Holland nodded.

'Their whole philosophy changed. If you've ever felt old...'

Holland nodded again. 'My hard-earned wisdom of age has been mistaken for doddering foolishness.'

'And mine was mistaken for dowdiness. I'd been there for thirty-eight years and seven months. But when they were aiming for different goals, all I'd done for them got lost in everybody's shuffle to dance to the new tune. I wasn't needed. I was in their way.'

'You've left Baseman Insurance?'

'Four months ago. I started working part-time for a small family firm of attorneys, doing legal research and trying to straighten up their antiquated bookkeeping system.'

'They like you,' he smiled.

'That's the good news. But I didn't get a golden parachute.'

'And the new firm isn't able to pay you as well. So there isn't any help in caring for your brother?'

'Well, there, at least, I have learned realistic goals. I found a couple who runs a small foster home, mostly for the elderly. They are gentle and patient and they've made James feel as though he is their helper with the old folks. In a real sense, I think he is. Maybe for the first time, he is the one giving and doing for others and he loves it. Sometimes he's got something lined up and he's reluctant to come home with me for the weekend. Maybe I'll end up moving in there with him,' she laughed, but Holland could see that that was her attempt at a joke she wasn't quite sure was funny.

'You're having to restart your life with two huge props knocked out from under your foundation.'

'I'm floundering,' she admitted. 'But for the first time in a long, long time I'm making decisions that include my welfare in the equations. It's new, but I think - I hope - it will be good. Somebody advised me to take a long vacation and set my own goals. But I remembered your telling me about the business executives who take a week at the beach before they can even think about slowing down. By the time they're ready to relax, the vacation time is over and they're flung back into the rat race.'

'So you're postponing yours?'

'Well, I have been thinking about it. And, you know, I'm getting so much enjoyment just in wondering about it, it's almost like that visualization trick you taught me last year. Just planning and picturing myself in a gondola on the Venice canals, or on the deck of a cruise ship in the Caribbean - just picturing myself doing something like that is precious. I don't want to jump into any of them until I've had all the fun of trying them all in my mind. Does that make sense?'

'It not only makes sense, it's the stuff of wisdom. You've hit on a treasure. But this year has been costly, hasn't it?'

'Oh, my, yes,' she sighed. And then she looked at him and a smile gave a pleasant intensity to the deep crows' feet at the edges of her eyes. 'But it's been worth it. James isn't a functioning adult, but he is functioning at the level he's capable of. And he's happy. And I'm happy. Oh, I hope to be happier as I search out ways to ease this burden I've been carrying for so very long. But there's peace within me that even money troubles aren't tearing apart.

'You know,' she suddenly leaned forward and laughed, 'that couple have been so pleased with the help James gives them that they've started paying him. Oh, it's just a couple dollars at the end of each week, but he's so proud to be earning money of his very own. And they've cut down on their bill to me for his care. They must have seen my cash problems, but they had the grace to say they've never hired a better assistant and are bribing me to make sure I don't take him away from them!'

'People can be so insightful.'

'But it's not just pity. It's real. Doctor, has help always been this close and I've never been able to see it before?'

He shook his head. 'None of us can reach and accept anything until we're ready, can we?'

'So the question is irrelevant, isn't it? What matters is that now I'm finally ready. And help is coming - in abundance.'

'And James is ready. He might not have been earlier. He needed your care and help to be able to see the needs of others. You've done a tremendous job, you know, pretty lady.'

'I do know,' she smiled. There was such deep joy in her face, no one could have looked at her without a smile of his own.

SHARE

Charlie wasn't a bitter young man. As the youngest of four close boys, he'd learned early to take what he got and make something out of it. He was born on Elmer's second birthday, so all his childhood he shared a birthday cake. It wasn't until he grew up and got married that he had a cake of his own. And that lasted only until the birth of his first daughter. Carolyn came on the day before his birthday, so the rest of his life he got crumbs.

Perhaps that's why when the Great Depression hit, he was the first of his family to get back on his feet. Not that he wasn't disappointed in the complete devastation of his dreams. He'd worked part time and put himself through college at Carnegie Tech as a lubrication engineer. He'd lined up a position with a large oil firm where he would start work as soon as he earned his degree.

But by the time graduation came, the oil companies were laying off workers with many years' seniority. There was no room on the payroll for a brand new engineer still wet behind the ears.

Charlie pressed thin lips together, took a deep breath and decided that the fault wasn't within himself but with the economy. He started looking for what was still open.

Several miles from his parents' home on steep Lilac Avenue, a gas station was struggling. Its owner needed night help, and Charlie would work anywhere, any time. He started running the station from late afternoon into the wee hours of the morning.

The owner had always been a spend-what-you've-got-in-your-pocket kind of guy. And these days there was next to nothing in his pocket.

Charlie had a little money and he was willing to work. He bought the station on time. At least that way the owner had something steady coming in and was free to try to find other work for himself.

'What are you doing to our reputation?' Charlie's three brothers asked. 'A gas station? We've always been steel people. Our dad is a ward officer and respected politician here in Pittsburgh. What do you think you are you doing?'

Charlie looked at them and shrugged. 'I'm eating,' he said.

They didn't deign to answer that one.

As the economy slid deeper and deeper, more and more men weren't eating - or feeding their families. The gas station wasn't making a mint and it needed long hours of constant work and care. But it was paying for the supplies and it was paying enough besides that Charlie could feed his secret bride, Alice. They'd eloped, but they couldn't tell anyone. Alice had not quite finished nurses' training. If her superiors found out that she was married, she would be dropped from the R.N. program despite the years she'd already put in.

'Uh, Charlie?' his brother said, drawing in the cinders of the back alley with the toe of his scuffed leather shoe.

Charles knew immediately what John needed. John had always been a little slow. But he was steady and reliable if you took the effort to explain clearly what you needed done. But he couldn't give you more than he had. And with so many able-bodied and able-minded men desperate for work, John had been laid off.

'I could use your help, John,' Charlie said, and it was almost true. He had been putting in fourteen and sixteen hour days seven days a week. He wouldn't be able to leave the station with only John in charge. But maybe he could snatch a couple hours sleep while John kept watch.

So John was the first of his brothers Charles hired. As the Depression worsened, Elmer and Arthur came, too. Reluctant rather than grateful, still they worked well part time and took their meager paychecks home to their wives. Arthur's wedding had been their mothers' delight. Elmer eloped and their parents were furious. Charlie and Alice didn't dare tell of their own quiet union.

At midnight, there isn't a lot of traffic so Charlie sent all of his brothers home. He was alone for the last two hours of the shift. Tonight had gone pretty well. He'd be able to pay for the new shipment of diesel and even send a little extra in John's check this week. That would get to Mother for Christmas preparations, of course, and that was exactly what Charlie intended. His father James was still a proud man and Charlie wanted to keep it that way as long as possible.

Charlie sat in the straight-backed chair wrapped in the afghan throw his mother had made for them. He tilted the chair onto the back two legs and stretched his long legs with his feet up on a stack of retread tires. From the wrinkled paper bag he drew out the bologna sandwich and set it on his thigh to unwrap the folded waxed paper.

He smiled at seeing how carefully Alice had tucked in the edges. She was a stickler for hospital corners on their bed sheets, too. At least she had been until he couldn't fit his six-foot one-inch frame within the confined space. From then on, she'd made sure his corner was tucked in loosely so he could push it out with only a slight movement of his feet.

The rap startled him. He hadn't seen any headlights of a car coming in. Charlie rocked forward so the chair stood on four legs. Charlie half-rose until he saw the wisp of a man at the doorway.

'Come in,' Charlie called and waved, then settled back into his chair. 'It's cold out there.'

'Aye, it is that,' the man said. His teeth chattered. He slumped on another stack of retread tires and sat rubbing his hands to get back the feeling in them. Every now and again he sidled a glance at the bologna half sandwich Charlie was eating.

Charlie gathered the other half in its waxed paper nest and reached across to hand it to the man. 'I hate to eat alone,' he said as though the man would be doing him a favor to join him in his meager meal.

Charlie knew from the way the claw-like hand lurched forward that this man hadn't eaten anything in some time. One bologna sandwich isn't much of a feast for a big man, and half is even less of one - unless it's shared with someone so nearly starved that he'd have been grateful to lick the crumbs from the slick paper.

'Do you like coffee?' Charlie asked. 'Black okay? I've got some sugar in a jar here somewhere...' He dug out the sweetener his brother Arthur always insisted on and the man poured nearly half of the contents of the jar into the mug of steaming brown-black fluid Charlie handed him. Part of the overspill was due to the shaking of his hands. Part, Charlie knew, was because the man simply craved as many calories as he could decently commandeer. Hunger has a way of ruling out over pride.

They sat a few minutes while the man devoured Charlie's liquid offering. When he'd drained off the mug, Charlie rocked forward again and emptied the thermos into the mug and held the jar of sugar out for him to take.

'Finish it up,' he said. 'I'll bring some from home in the morning. Then stay here a while until you get warm. I've got some stock to put away before I close up.'

Gray-blue eyes flashed a look of gratitude and envy, then immediately the hawk-like face looked down again, concentrating on pouring sugar from the jar. He was bird-like, this gaunt man in what had once been a fairly decent wool overcoat. The boots were large for the long feet, the metal buckles closed tight but still the dark rubber picked up an instant after the leg and foot had lifted.

'I've got some old newspaper,' Charlie said handing him the front section of the Pittsburgh rag from two days ago. A motorist had dumped it beside the pump and Elmer had wanted to throw it out after he looked over the financial section. But Charlie had had John pick it up and smooth it out and stack it under the counter. 'Might keep the feet warmer if you wrap it around your shoes.'

'What shoes?' the man mumbled almost incoherently so it was only after Charlie was out in the cold that he realized what had been said.

Methodically, Charlie gathered the sign and cans and boxes and brought them in to stack them beside the door to be carried out again in the morning - just five hours from now.

The man sat hunkered into the retreads, his chin on his chest, breathing regularly as though asleep. But still he clawed the mug, though there was only a trace of coffee tilted in its bottom.

'Oh, well, let him sleep until I get the proceeds into the safe and finish securing everything,' Charlie decided. 'It'll be hard enough to turn him out into the snow then.'

Naturally cautious after surviving childhood with three older brothers, Charlie glanced over at the visitor before opening the cash box, but he didn't stir.

Satisfied, Charlie counted the day's intake - just about enough to meet expenses - and carried the box to the narrow door in the back, off the garage. The basement steps were as steep as a twenty-foot wooden ladder tilted to cover the eighteen feet to the cement floor below.

Charlie had never been afraid of heights. He'd scared his mother, and even his father, on the steep-pitched roof of the house more than once. He scrambled down face forward and crossed among the boxes of tire chains and barrels of oil to a safe that was a good decade older than he was. He set the cash box on top and bent to twist the dial. Left two full turns, stop at 7...

What warned him, Charlie was never sure. There was light only from one dim bulb hanging from the ceiling near the base of the stairs so there couldn't have been much of a shadow. Maybe it was a sound as the man raised the tire chain. But if there was a clink of metal it was too soft for Charlie to register as a separate sound. In the moment it took Charlie to twist to avoid the blow, Charlie saw as he turned that the man had wound the chain around his arm so only the short section he was about to use as a weapon was left free to jangle.

Charlie felt the wrack of heavy chain, but he'd taken most of it on his left shoulder. By now he was crouched and turned. He sprang, ramming his right shoulder into the man's chest, driving him backward into a barrel.

Half-starved and fully three inches shorter than Charlie, his only chance had been surprise. It might have worked. But it didn't. Charlie pummeled the man, driving him to the cold cement. If the man hadn't fought, Charlie would have merely pinned him there with his knee in his chest. But the man, fingers still sticky with sugar grains, clawed at his face.

Charlie gave him a right jab that brought a spurt of blood to his nose. 'Leave off!' Charlie commanded, and finally he did.

He moaned once, then went still. But those blue-gray eyes looked up with a hatred that made Charlie want to hit him again.

'What in the world? I even gave you my supper!'

Then Charles eased his weight slowly from the frail chest.

'Get out of here,' he said, still angrier than he been except a very few times in his life. 'Beat it! But don't ever let me catch sight of you again.'

He towered over the figure gathering himself, scrambling backwards until he could drag himself to his feet. The blue-gray eyes flashed once more, but the message was deeper and more complex than Charlie could read.

Charlie rubbed his aching shoulder as he watched the figure scrabble up the wooden stairs. He shook his head.

'I've never been that hungry,' he whispered.

JO ◯

It's the day-to-day stuff that grinds you down. Especially when the day starts at 1 AM.

Groaning, Jo turned over in her lonely bed and attacked the battered alarm clock. Somebody has to go out and get the irrigation system up and going. It's your golf course, Jo. That means the somebody is you.

She'd found high school boys who would do it faithfully for a while. But as they learned how draining it was they'd find excuses to do it less and less often. Not that she could blame them. True, on summer nights the stars create a canopy of celestial hope. But their nurturing perspective fades as dawns wear into endless days of demands she couldn't possibly fulfill. And midnight fog or chill or wind can sap your courage. The howl of a roving coyote can put ice in crevices of your spine you didn't even know you had.

They'd started with such high hopes, the four of them. Moving from the bleakness of Utah to lush Oregon had seemed more of an adventure than a gamble how many years ago? Two couples who had been friends forever, who had worked golf courses and played golf well enough to consider turning pro, they'd seen the advertisements for the little nine-holer west of Portland. 'This is it!' they'd grinned at each other. They hadn't much money, but they had sweat and determination and know-how. They could make this little course into something to be proud of. It was perfect.

But nothing is ever perfect.

The people were good old farmers and small town folk. They weren't extravagant, but they were patient when they saw how faithfully the four worked the land. That kind of devoted building, these people could understand and applaud, in their own undemonstrative way.

But equipment got old and required elaborate tinkering. Water rates were raised. A fire broke out in the garage and the groundsman risked his life racing into the blaze to save the truck. They couldn't decide whether to thank him for the truck or scold him for putting his life in jeopardy.

A teenager ran into the telephone pole beside the two-lane highway that parallels the first fairway. Their small town mourned, including Jo's growing sons.

The daily chores wore Jo's husband down. He started downing a beer now and again to settle him. He wasn't a pleasant drunk, except with the customers. At home, well, it wasn't how she'd planned to live her married life, and it sure was taking a toll on the boys. Like father, like son. How do you convince a child that parts of his beloved dad shouldn't be emulated?

Setbacks hurt them financially, but those they could deal with. It was the relationships that were being torn apart. The partners, reluctant to break up the friendship, tried one tact and then another. Finally they opted out. Jo couldn't blame them. She knew how hard they'd tried. But it left the care of the course which had been a task for four now to two. And the money got even tighter. They'd asked to be bought out. The money was theirs, after all. But, oh, money was tight.

The divorce was finally Jo's idea, in self-defense. It meant she was no longer being attacked, but it also meant she was alone in charge of the whole course.

One AM. Time to rise. Time to slide into her slacks and sweatshirt and wool socks. Time to stumble downstairs murmuring thanks that the automated irrigation system would soon be functional. 'No more middle-of-the-night shifts!' she murmured gleefully. 'Oh, boy, that'll be the day!'

It had been a huge decision. It was a huge expense, but bare feet on the wooden floor each one AM weighed in the balance. 'I'm a born optimist, I guess,' Jo sighed, struggling into her Pacific Northwest down jacket. 'That sprinkling system will pay for itself in no time.'

But she'd already run the figures. By the time it had paid for itself, it would long since have needed repairs and/or replacement.

Still, things were going pretty well. People had by-and-large understood when she'd had to raise the annual fee. They understood rising expenses and knew her course was still the best value for the walker. It was the social setting for many of the retirees of the area. She didn't insist on strict golfing rules or etiquette. These tough old men had their own rules, and it was a decent society so she let them work things out their way.

Jo crunched her way across the frosted grass plot between the back of the house and the clubhouse. The security light was on, but its powerful beam played mostly on the public area. Jo walked in shadow to the little door to the locker room. An errant Santa leered at her from above the end cubby where the Sagars cached their golf shoes and clubs. She'd have to remember to get him down. People were looking forward to the New Year.

Brrrr, it was cold in here. The thermostat was set low for the night, but Jo couldn't remember 55 feeling quite this cold - or drafty.

The hairs on the back of neck pricked. She stopped in the shadow of the four-foot wall between the lockers and the gathering area with its long tables. Most of the room was in shadow, but the security light etched out eerie triangles in what was totally familiar in the daylight. Frightened, Jo shivered and held her breath. Every instinct told her to bolt and run.

'This is your livelihood, lady,' she scolded. 'And the way you're helping your kids through college. If there's something wrong, you better find out what it is. The sooner fixed, the cheaper.'

Jo slipped into the shadow in the corner of the gathering room and peered around. The tables were askew. The one closest had been pushed against the partition wall. Jo lifted her eyes. The big screen TV where the guys sat drinking coffee and watching golfing matches - it was gone!

How could someone misplace that huge screen?

Even as Jo faced the double door that led to the Eighth tee, she knew she wasn't being rational. The TV had been stolen, and recently. Tonight. The old wooden doors hung open, their windows shattered and unable to keep out the cold even if the thieves had been polite and closed them as they left.

Jo sucked air.

'Oh, Lord, not again. Not another loss and hassle with the police and the insurance.' She frowned. 'Speaking of loss,' she said and stared across the end of the room past the coffee urn toward her counter. The till. The whole cash register. Gone!

She froze, catching sight of movement outside.

'Oh!' she whispered and shrank back into the shadows to watch along the walkway in front of the metal barn where the electric golfcarts were stored.

Black figures moved in and out of bleak patches of light.

She ducked and crawled to the phone. '9-1-1,' she whispered, 'call the police!'

She gave the operator the information as quickly and quietly as she could. And then she huddled there feeling violated. Again. 'Enough, please,' she whispered.

Jo had no idea how long she stayed there, waiting. Waiting for the thieves to come back to punish her for having called the cops. Waiting for the 'happily ever after' she'd assumed in her naivete would be the comfort of her marriage. Waiting for her children to run to her rescue, though she knew they were safely away from all of this, busy building the foundations of their own lives. She could only hope their dreams would find a gentler path than hers had found.

She was startled by Dave's call from the front door. 'Jo! Jo, are you okay?'

'Here,' she squeaked, and suddenly her chief of operations was there to lift her to her feet and help her stumble into the gathering room to sit at the nearest table.

A policeman was right behind him. It was a small community. They'd known to notify Dave for her.

'Hi, Jim,' Dave said. 'She wasn't seen. She wasn't hurt, just shaken.'

'And shaking,' Jim acknowledged with a smile. 'It's chilly in here.'

'Yeah,' Dave said. 'I'll get some plywood and block those windows. Okay if I close these doors?'

'Let me dust for fingerprints,' Jim said.

At Jim's nod, Dave eased the two sides of the double door together, carefully avoiding touching the knobs. On his way out, he stopped to set the coffee maker to brewing.

As Jim finished at the door and interior furnishings, including the counter where the cash register had sat, he saw that the coffee was ready. He motioned for Jo to wait while he brought her coffee, but she shook her head and got up.

'Okay,' he said, realizing her need to reclaim some semblance of order and control. He sat at the table nearest the window overlooking the ninth fairway and green. She was bringing two steaming Styrofoam cups when he got the call on his cell phone. 'Okay, he nodded into the phone, then, 'Thanks. I'll tell her.'

'What? Did they find them?'

'Yes, and no. One good thing about crime in a farming community. If it happens at night, there aren't a lot of other vehicles out to muddy up the search.'

'They found their truck?'

'Yep, it was reported stolen earlier tonight. We gave chase, but the thieves drove like sixty until they put the truck into a ditch. I'm afraid your stuff got mangled.'

'What about the thieves?'

'They took off running in three different directions. Didn't catch up with any of them, I'm afraid. Sorry.'

Jo lowered her head. She'd wanted them caught, but they'd been seen and chased, and even that was more than she could have asked for. She wouldn't get the use of her things again, but at least they wouldn't get anything out of all this, either.

'Well, thanks for coming so fast. We came awfully close.'

Jo sat down across from Jim and sipped at her own cup of comfort.

'It's the daily grind that gets you down,' she murmured, 'but the occasional moments of terror and loss can polish you off.'

'If you let them,' Jim agreed. He knew about her courage in keeping Sunset going all these years. 'Hey, what in the blue blazes is that?' he asked when Dave returned and switched on the overhead lights on his way to the double doors.

'What? The mobile?'

'I can see it's a mobile. With what? little bugs? floating around globs?'

'Bees,' Jo said. The kids made bees for me from pipe cleaners and bits of paper and glue.'

'So what are the globs?'

'Ummyom,' Dave explained, then explained again with the nails out of his mouth. 'Honeycomb. See that wall next to where you're sitting? Bees got in under that window and built a colony. The honey finally started oozing through. We had to take out the inside wall and patch up where they were getting in and then redo that whole portion of the wall and repaint. It was some job.'

'Good honey?' Jim asked.

'Oh, yeah. And Jo here decided we needed a reminder of the tough times and how we always get through them somehow. She worked for days stringing and balancing until those bits of comb finally hung pretty level and she had me hang that mobile right over where the TV screen used to be.'

'Now I understand,' Jim laughed as he saluted her. 'I've often wondered how you could keep this place going what with everything that's happened. Courage.'

'Stubbornness,' Jo managed.

'Sometimes it amounts to the same thing. It's a good thing the thieves didn't know to take your brown badge of courage, too,' Jim laughed, pointing at the mobile.

Dave pounded in the last nail and turned to shrug. 'She'd have built another one.' Both men grinned.

ENEMY ID

Del had been on enough burglary and breaking-and-entering cases that he knew to wait out the angry construction boss still boiling over at his question.

'How do I know when the jerk came?' the man growled. 'We work like dogs and go home dog-tired past sundown. And only then because we're as likely to pound a nail into our hands as into a 2 x 4.' He clenched his right fist, evidently in remembered pain.

'But you locked up last night?' Del asked over his notebook. He looked up when there wasn't any answer. The construction boss stood flat-footed, the extended fingers of his left hand closing and opening again.

'Hey,' Del said hastily, 'I just need your affirmation for my report. It makes a difference on what we can charge the guy with.'

'IF you find him - and can prove anything.'

'Assuming that, yeah,' Del agreed. 'So you always lock up at night...'

'You think I'd leave my whole operation open for anybody and his uncle to come along and steal? This is my livelihood. I got three kids.'

'Me, too,' Del said. For a minute, Del was afraid he was going to fight him on this, too. But something seemed to soften inside the man. 'Two of the prettiest girls you've ever seen. And my boy.'

'Two boys,' the man nodded, 'but I think I'd go toe to toe with you about how pretty a girl can be.'

Del grinned. And thanked God and his parents for that grin. It had broken down more barriers than all the police techniques he'd been taught. Not that he wanted to do without any of them. He'd needed them a time or two, as well.

The construction boss didn't grin, but he did wipe his right hand against his pant leg and extend it, partly open. 'Stu Marvin,' he said.

Flipping his notebook and ballpoint into his left hand, Del grasped the man's hand. It hadn't been opened totally for him because it couldn't be, Del realized from the thick, clawing scar tissue.

'Del Konschu. Sorry to meet you in lousy circumstances like this.'

Stu's face hardened again. 'Lousy foul-ups,' he muttered.

'You think you know who did this?' Del twisted open the notebook again.

'Nah, nothing as useful as that. But this is the third time on this job I been busted into. Insurance don't want to pay, but they sure want enough from me, and I can't afford to go without.'

'And they set the rates so you can hardly afford to hang onto it,' Del nodded. Indeed he did know about insurance. But he hadn't seen a file yet, so he hadn't known about the other two break-ins. 'Any luck finding the other two perps?'

'Nothing they could hang on them.' Stu shrugged. 'So now I gotta get back to making a living for them, too. See how quick you can get this paperwork overwith so I can use my office, will you?'

'In a minute, Stu.' Del had almost called him Mr. Marvin, as he'd been trained. But he knew instinctively that Stu would bristle. He was close to doing that again right now. 'Stu, I've learned to look around outside before any clues out here get trampled. I've caught a couple from odd shoe casts I was able to find. Give me a minute out here before we go inside, will you?'

Stu lowered his head with a snort, but when he looked up, he met Del's eyes. He nodded once and thrust his fists into his pockets, the picture of neither resignation nor patience. But he'd shaken hands. He'd go along for a little while. The littler the better.

Nodding his thanks, Del stuffed his notebook into his pocket and walked carefully in a wide circle, studying the ground and the surroundings. It was a typical construction site: mud, elderly heavy equipment, dirty, sweating men with bulging arm muscles, tight lips and squinting eyes. One, a young, skinny one with his hardhat dangling from a hook on his belt, sidled up to the battered, once-green trailer that served as the office.

'Back off!' Stu Marvin snapped.

The youth stopped dead just outside the first of Del's circles. He looked from Stu to Del and back again, shrugged and sauntered off as though he'd only come to do them a favor anyway.

Del glanced over to thank Stu for protecting his territory, but he was met with hard, angry eyes. Clearly Stu thought he was being used - again.

Del scanned just as carefully, but his circles were smaller and smaller as he neared the trailer's door. A padlock hung, ruptured and useless. The metal door looked ready for retirement, but it hadn't been only from this latest insult. Many dents were caved and rusty. That door had taken long years of beating.

Del turned and signaled to Stu that he was going inside.

'No need for plaster of Paris?' Stu's called taunt both voiced his frustration and dated him.

Rather than antagonize the man further, Del merely shook his head and, pushing the door with the end of notebook to avoid smearing any prints, stepped up and inside. Using the notebook that way was more from habit than hope. The metal door was smeared with layers upon layers of dirt, smudged, smeared and probably useless to the police.

'Oh, boy,' Del breathed as he stepped inside. He'd had the idea these men were too busy for neatness. Stu had already admitted he didn't have time even to keep inventory. He had no idea what had been taken - and no way to figure it out. Unless he or one of the men missed something, it was simply gone. There'd be no tracing stolen goods if they didn't have a description of what had been stolen. The mess of the place could have been the men's own doing as well as that of the thief.

But Del was thorough if he was anything. Methodical. His occasional partners were usually exasperated with him long before he was finished studying a crime scene. Stuffing the notebook back into his pocket, Del went through the motions, studying every square foot of the trailer's interior, looking for who knew what. He took a half dozen photos, but he knew before they were developed that they wouldn't be any use as evidence.

The telephone was toward the back end of the trailer, on a cluttered metal desk stacked high with papers in lopsided piles that spilled onto each other. At least some of that mess must have been made by the thief. Del stood a minute staring. What was wrong with this picture? A section of neatness intruded upon the pattern of chaos.

Lying precisely in front of the squared-up phone was an open wallet with a scrap of unfolded paper laid out and smoothed exactly over the exposed plastic photo sleeves. On that paper was a name and address in Paris, and a phone number.

'Oh, no,' Del breathed. It couldn't be. He snapped a close-up.

'Stu!' he called and Marvin was instantly at the doorway, peering in. 'You got your wallet?'

'Yeah,' the man growled, but his left hand went to the hip pocket of his jeans. 'Yeah,' he answered with a little less edginess. 'Why? What you got?' He started to hitch up and in, but Del waved him back.

Del stepped closer to read the name on the driver's license inside its plastic cover.

'Any of your guys named...?' He read the name out, pronouncing distinctly. He didn't want any mistakes here.

'Nah,' Stu started, but Del interrupted sharply.

'Ask them!' he ordered and again pronounced the name with exaggerated preciseness.

It was too good to be true, but for once it was true.

'I think you're going to find a call to France on your phone bill, Mr. Marvin,' Del said, trying to keep himself from smiling.

'What? France? I don't know nobody in France...? You're kidding!'

Del had stepped to one side so Stu could see the wallet in plain sight on the desk.

'The perp?' Stu guffawed. 'Maybe there is Justice up there in the skies. That's too much!'

It took a few minutes for Del to finish photographing the evidence in place and satisfy himself there was nothing else incriminating before he scooped up the wallet and slid it into an evidence bag.

He had a hearty handshake from Stu and a couple of the others as he made his way back to his patrol car.

'No need for plaster of Paree this time, Del?' Stu laughed. 'Looks like he cast his own one-way ticket this time.'

Del called in with what he'd found and advised Central that he was on his way to the address on the driver's license. It was on his way, after all, and only a few blocks from the jail.

'Backup on the way,' they advised him.

He parked at the end of the driveway, blocking easy escape. He walked quietly up onto the porch and knocked at the screen door.

A burly man with his T-shirt tucked precisely into his jeans came and stood staring at him through the mesh. He craned to look out at the patrol car and then met Del's eyes.

103

'Yeah, that's me,' he answered, suspicious, but he opened the screen door at Del's gesture.

'Might you have misplaced your wallet, Sir?'

The man's eyes widened. Even as he shook his head and denied having lost it, his hand went to his empty pocket. His eyes narrowed.

'Oh, man. The call.'

'I'm afraid you'll have to come with me, Sir.'

'Where to?'

'Not nearly as far as Paris, Sir. The county jail is only just down the street.'

GRINDING DOWN

Wayne was a seasoned veteran in the California Highway Patrol. He rode his motorcycle into situations that would have made Evel Kneivel blanch. But for Wayne, it was a matter of professional pride not to talk about his exploits. A crooked smile, a flick of a wrist as though to toss off any special significance for what he'd done day in, and day out, on the murderous freeways of Los Angeles: That's all anyone ever got in response to pleas for tales of his often hazardous duty as a law enforcement officer.

Until Juanita mentioned The Chase. Those of us listening could hear the capital letters. We sat up around Wally's coffee table spread for celebration of his hole-in-one. We glanced at each other. Maybe this time we'd hear something from our retired friend and golfing buddy.

'Come on, Wayne! What happened in The Chase?' we begged.

He glowered at Juanita, but Wayne could never deny his animated wife anything, even a claim to his carefully guarded story.

'It wasn't much,' he started slowly, 'but I guess there aren't a whole lot of stories just like it.'

We gathered closer. Wayne was a big man, but he spoke softly.

'We'd gotten a call on the radio. Armed robbery. Detailed description of the get-away car, including the license plate number. We didn't often get that much to go on, so I was pretty sure the guy'd be picked up. I remember hoping for a moment that it'd be me that got him. You like to think you're doing your bit.'

Gary added another black olive to his paper plate of tiny sandwiches and sat in the nearest chair. 'Did you get your wish?'

'And then some,' Wayne nodded.

'You've got to be careful what you wish for,' Barbara chuckled, but her bright cheerleader eyes narrowed in concern.

'Amen to that,' Juanita agreed so fervently that we grew even quieter. This was going to be some kind of tale.

'You spotted the get-away car,' Earl guessed, and Wayne nodded.

'I was pretty sure from the description of the car and of the blond kid in the baseball cap, so I radioed in that I was closing in to check the license plate. I sort of eased up on him without getting too close. I didn't want to spook him before patrol cars could get into place ahead of us. We were coming up on the junction of I-5 and I-10 and there were a lot of possible ways he could go. It would be better to see which way he was going before we tried to close in on him.'

'But he saw you,' Wally guessed, and Wayne grimaced.

'I guess if he'd just committed a crime, his guilt would make him sure any cop within visual range was after him,' Barbara said.

'It would make me hypersensitive, that's for sure,' Gary agreed.

Wayne glanced at his audience of friends, smiling at their support. 'Whatever,' he said low, but it was clear that he still blamed himself for spooking the suspect. 'At any rate, just as I was confirming the license number, he suddenly took off like a bat out of wherever.'

He glanced around again. For as tough as his world had been, he still had the gentleman's reluctance to speak roughly in the company of women.

Juanita sidled closer and put her manicured hand on his arm.

'You took off after him,' Gary prompted.

'Oh, yeah,' Wayne breathed. His chin lowered, then raised. He looked at his friends. His shoulders straightened to fill out his pale blue golf shirt. We had the feeling this might be the first time he'd actually enjoyed telling the story. It was like watching a load of years of duty being, at last, retired from those shoulders.

'It's always terrifying on a freeway chase,' Wayne related, clearly warming to his yarn-spinning. 'The traffic is going so fast. There's always the real possibility of a high-impact crash and innocent civilians getting hurt. The little Dodge Dart swept into the on-ramp for I-10 going east. That's the San Bernardino. It was only a few minutes before I could hear sirens, and I guess he could hear them, too. He stopped zipping in and out between startled drivers and slithered off the Atlantic exit at the last second. Another couple bike lengths and I wouldn't have been able to follow him. That was a hairy turn,' Wayne said, shaking his head. 'Oh, yeah, I remember that one. But the adrenaline gets pumping. The sirens are on. Your lights are flashing. All you want to do is get this guy.'

He was quiet for a moment and none of us interrupted. When he swallowed and looked at us, he was grinning.

'Atlantic was pretty quiet for that part of town. It was early afternoon and most of even the long-lunchers were already back at work. There was traffic, though. We were going too fast for people ahead to have time to hear and pull over. But this blond kid was passing everybody like they were standing still. A couple times he didn't leave much more than a coat of paint between them when he squeezed back in ahead of oncoming traffic. A few times he took some souvenir paint, but so far he was doing pretty slick.

'And then, almost like in the movies, there was a construction site with a cement mixer taking up the curb lane and a good bit more.' Wayne wiped his palms down the thighs of his chino pants.

'I could hear sirens behind me and thought I could make out at least one coming toward us, but I'd have had to do what I did even if it meant losing the kid.'

Now it was Wally and Gary wiping their own palms. Barbara clutched her china cup and sat down in the Queen Victoria chair.

'The cement guy came storming out, screaming at the kid's close run past his truck. The sluice was still shimmying. I guess the guy heard all the sirens and didn't pick out where mine was coming from. He stepped directly in front of me, turned away to cuss after the kid in the Dodge Dart.

'I laid that bike down in the quickest left turn I've ever made in my life. I didn't think. I just reacted. I didn't even feel the bike go down. I was gunning it past the mixer, and then the next second I was down on the macadam and gravel and still plowing south, this time without the bike. I could hear it screech across the road and the crash and burn when it slammed into a car parked on the other side. But there I was, still sailing south on Atlantic!

'I was riding my hind end. I was all drawn up, like folded in the middle so my arms and head were up and my feet were up and nothing on the macadam but my nether parts, as Juanita puts it. It was funny. I wasn't hurting but I knew I would be in a little while. Still there was this suspended moment when traffic coming toward me was climbing the curb to get out of my way. I could hear the sirens. I could even see the Dodge Dart being corralled at the far end of the block. Talk about a moment in time feeling like a week or two!

'And all that time I was waiting for the pain. Actually hoping for a little of it after a while, because it began to dawn on me that maybe I'd snapped my spine and I wouldn't be able to move or feel anything ever again.

'Finally I slowed and slowed. My legs lowered. My trunk flattened out and all I could do was keep my chin tucked to keep my head up off the road. And then I stopped. For a long minute all I could do was lie there and work at breathing. I don't think I'd taken in any air at all for the whole ride on my butt.

'I was lying there heaving in the street and I couldn't believe I was still alive, let alone that I wasn't hurting to beat the band. I hadn't hit anything. And nothing had hit me. I'd just skidded, uncontrolled, for half a block and all I had to show was some gravel and road burns.

'I rolled onto my side before anybody could get to me, still wondering why my bottom wasn't screaming at me. And it was only then that I realized that my holster had gotten twisted on my hip. I'd been riding leather. I hiked up and tugged the belt around to look. I'd been riding that holster all right. You could see the scraping so the part over the chamber of the gun was so thin it was only Juanita's prayer holding it together.'

Wayne stopped and looked down at his wife huddled into his shoulder.

'Oh, Wayne, you never told me all of it like that,' she breathed.

'It's okay,' he told her low. 'It all came out all right in the end.'

'Oh, Wayne!'

MILLIE'S FIGHT

'You can't do anything, then, Doc?' Millie asked of the Oregon Health Sciences University ophthalmologist.

He shook his head. Knowing his patient couldn't see the dejected movement, he said quietly, 'I'm afraid not, Millie. We've exhausted all possibilities.'

'I'm a fighter,' Mildred told him, long fingers splayed and flashing in the air for emphasis. 'When my husband was gone, I finished my nurse's training to be able to support myself and my little girl. My sister Inez helped me raise her and when Inez took ill for the last years of her life, who do you think cared for her day after day, month after month?'

'I'm sure you did a wonderful job with her.'

'I'm not fishing for compliments. I'm asking you to give me something to fight for. Some light at the end of the tun...'

Millie stopped, her mouth open. As her daughter Betty watched with an aching heart, Millie's mouth closed slowly into its determined thin line.

'That was almost funny,' she breathed.

'Almost,' he agreed. His voice was strained. No matter how many years he'd been an eye doctor, he'd never learned to be unfeeling at these moments.

'This is the end of the tunnel, isn't it?' Mildred said. 'And there is no light.'

'You still have that lamp you can make out in your living room, don't you? It must be a great help in orienting yourself in your apartment. It's a good thing you were able to stay in your own place as you dealt with your growing blindness.'

'Umm,' she murmured, but she was shaking her head so the white medium length straight hair flopped to one side and then the other. Mildred drew in her long fingers - so good at crocheting and quilting - and closed them into small fists.

She'd had a light. A small table lamp in the living room of her one-floor duplex gave a tiny light that she could see. She used it as a beacon for orientation. No one knew why that particular lamp was visible when others brighter or dimmer didn't penetrate the darkness that had grown to consume her over the last few years. But last month even its feeble glow had been snuffed. Mildred lived in blackness. She'd held onto the hope that the doctors could come up with something to relieve the blindness, but there was no hope.

She sighed, and then she did something few of his patients did. Mildred brought those tiny fists up and pounded them on the table between them. Mildred was a fighter.

'Okay, why do I have to have those eye drops every morning and night? What's the point if I'm not going to be able to see anyway?'

'Treating your eyes won't bring back your vision,' he explained. 'But one of the three conditions that blinded you is severe glaucoma. If we don't keep the channels open for the inner fluid to circulate, it will accumulate and the pressure will eventually give you pain. A lot of pain.'

That was the one explanation that made sense. 'Okay,' Mildred said and rose to go. The doctor watched her leave on Betty's arm. She was small, with a bent back and bony features, but she was a woman of courage. She'd make the rest of her life count, too.

Back in her duplex, Millie wasn't so sure. She kept the routine going. With Betty coming at least twice a day to administer the eyedrops and to line things up, Mildred was determined to stay in her own home for as long as she possibly could. The only trouble was, the days were long. She couldn't crochet or quilt any more. She really couldn't go anywhere unless someone came to get her and take her along. Many friends did, but still there were days after days when the hours dragged on. Even Mildred could listen to only so many sports presentations and soap operas.

'I think if I could get someone to take me, I'd consider jumping off the Interstate Bridge,' she muttered. And then she chuckled. 'I'd have to find someone who would drive me to Portland, let me out at the middle of the bridge, put my hand on the rail and then drive away and not look back. I don't know anybody that naïve. Maybe it's good that I can't think of one person that much of an enemy - or a friend.'

She sighed and coughed and picked up the remote and scanned the line-up of buttons with her thumb. There, that ought to mute the silly thing a minute. Now what was it she'd been hearing in the background?

Ah, the little overhead fire alarm. That thing again. Just about every time she put a heavy load into the dryer, that thing started screaming. Mildred concentrated a moment, trying to hear the rhythmic roar of the dryer working. Yes, it was still going. She could just pick it out between the annoying, piercing screeches of the alarm. She was going to have to ask grandsons Ben and Chad to simply take out the batteries so it wouldn't keep going off like that.

Mildred coughed again. It was getting warm. Millie loved warmth. Some overly helpful visitor must have turned up the thermostat without telling her. She coughed again. All those years of smoking had taken their toll. It was only been in the last couple months that Millie had given up her cigarettes for fear she'd leave one lighted and start a fire.

'Fire!'

The voices were close - inside the apartment, probably at the front door at the other end of the kitchen. Mildred lifted and turned in her chair as the voices came closer.

'Who's there?' Millie called. 'Is that you, Melody?'

'Fire, Millie! Your house is on fire!'

'What? What are you talking about? That alarm goes off half the time I have the dryer going. Who is it?'

'It's me, Melody, and my brother Alan from across the street.' Their words tumbled over each other's making it hard for Millie to grasp what they were saying. They were good kids. Sometimes Betty paid them to come to see to her needs when she couldn't make it over on a particular evening. But they certainly were wound up this morning.

Mildred coughed. 'Hey, slow down. I can't make head nor tails of what you're babbling about.' She felt one of them paw at her arm.

'Get up! We've got to get out of here!' Melody cried and then what she was saying got lost in her coughing.

Alan's strong young hands lifted Mildred from the chair and stood her on her feet. 'Millie, listen! We could see flames bursting out your bedroom window,' he said. 'Your apartment is on fire! You've got to get out - now!'

His coughing and Melody's moan of fear finally penetrated Mildred's denial.

'Flames from my bedroom?'

'Yeah! We saw them from across the street. Melody's already called 9-1-1, but we were afraid you wouldn't be able to get out in time. Come on!'

'Oh, God, Alan, come on where?' Melody screamed. 'I can't see a thing!'

'The smoke was bad enough when we came in here. Now I can't see anything either. How do we get out?'

'I'm all turned around. Oh, Lord, I don't even know where the door is. We're not going to make it!'

Mildred set her long fingers on Alan's arm. 'You can't see?'

'No!'

'Then follow me,' Millie ordered. 'I'm in the dark all the time. Come on, I'll get us out of here.'

The would-be rescuers followed Mildred as she led them outside to safety just as the fire trucks arrived. Later the fire inspectors determined that one of the covers from Mildred's bed had slid off onto the baseboard heater and smoldered there until it finally caused the blaze that gutted her one-bedroom duplex. All of Forest Grove and especially Mildred's family and friends praised the courage of the two young people from across the street who had risked their lives to save her.

But Alan and Melody were grateful to Mildred for leading them out of danger. And Mildred, though she didn't speak of it, never again thought much about the Interstate Bridge. She'd been needed, and, even blind, she'd come through, fighter as she was.

ALPINE WWII

'And I thought boot camp was tough!' Will leaned back into the corner of the deep sofa that marked off a hallway between kitchen and living area in the open mountain cabin on Mt. Hood. He sighed. 'Which it was. It was the 1940's and there wasn't time for frills or coddling. You had to be trained to go to war, as quickly as possible. But this - this was next to impossible.'

Ted dropped his eyes from the battered wooden skis hung crossed high on the tilted wall of the A-frame. He stared at Dr. A. 'Skiing was impossible?'

'No, Ted, skiing is and was incredible. There is no feeling like the wind and the chill and the rhythm of your flexed knees responding to the ground flying under your feet.'

'Flying?' Ted glanced back up at the straight skis with their heavy metal and leather bindings.

'Well, you're only just beginning. Six years old is a little small to be flying yet, but you will be soon, and then you'll have more fun than you ever dreamed was possible. It's pretty good now, too, isn't it?' Will smiled, aware of how kids hated to be told they were too little to understand yet.

'Oh, yeah!' Ted nodded, then brushed back his red hair with hands still grimy from the fireplace embers he and his sisters had used to make the face on their snowman.

'How come they let you ski, Dr. A? You were a soldier, weren't you? Weren't you supposed to fight?'

'Good question, Kathi,' Will smiled at my older daughter, just twelve now. 'It's seems hard to believe, but we were fighting. Skiing and fighting. The Army had sent us to the Alps as soldiers. We carried rifles wrapped in white cloth and big white packs strapped to our backs. Hard to believe the war would bring us to some of the best skiing in the whole world, but it had to make it tough, too, I suppose.'

'Tough? How?' Kathi's eyes were sparkling with love of zooming down the slopes, the snow stinging her cheeks.

'Well, for one thing, if the enemy had seen us...'

'So that's why the rifles were wrapped in white cloth!'

'Oh, yes, if anything dark showed up against the snow, it alerted them. Our suits were white, everything we could make white. And we skied at night.'

'With the lights on?' Ted asked, his mouth open.

Will laughed aloud, then quieted, remembering that his wife and son had just gotten to bed.

'No lights, Tedder,' Kathi said. 'They didn't want to be seen or they'd be shot.'

'Oh,' Ted frowned. 'But, wouldn't the white stuff show up in the dark?'

'Very good question,' Will nodded approval. 'But even in the dark in the Alps, any moonlight reflects off the snow and white is still your best camouflage color.'

'But couldn't you stay in the shadows of the trees?' Kathi asked. 'I sure wouldn't want to be caught out on the slope where some sniper might see me.'

'But - but you'd be skiing in the dark,' Alisa exclaimed. 'How could you see?'

Will peered at them. 'You've hit on what made it so hard. A lot of the time, we couldn't see. And it wasn't like the slopes here on Mt. Hood where they smooth it out with the big snow cats.'

His eyes drifted to look far beyond the A-frame's walls, far across the width of the United States and the Atlantic Ocean to southern Europe of thirty-five years before.

White backpack strap rubbing painfully into his left shoulder, Will whipped into the shadow of an evergreen and stopped to peer around him before struggling with the strap.

He hated the thought of dying without knowing what was coming. To die violently was simply a fact of war, but to die without seeing it coming, somehow that fretted at him. He slipped off the goggles for a minute the better to reach around to his shoulder to adjust the back without taking it off. He'd be too vulnerable if he had to unload all the gear and start over. Better to do what he could and put up with the discomfort rather than leave himself in a position where he couldn't ski off the instant he sensed danger. It was hell to pay, this skiing at night in the spring Alps. Ice melted and whole floes shifted, ripping apart snowfields so deep and wide you thought they would go on forever. Sudden cracks appeared in the surface, cracks that could be ten or twenty or fifty feet wide and hundreds of feet deep.

Skiing the Alps at night demands the skills of a trained athlete. 'Still, I'm in peak condition, thanks to the United States Army,' Will told himself as he shifted and tightened the offending strap. 'I'm on top of the world, almost literally.' Will Asbury grinned as he peered out at the slopes and up at the nearly round moon. If he was going to be killed, he couldn't think of a better vista in which to die.

He readjusted the goggles and peered out again, as he had been trained. Methodically, he scanned each degree of field. It was always an 'adventure' to venture out from cover.

'Here goes,' he muttered.

'I pushed off and ducked out from under that tree,' Will told the children, his mind now back inside his mountain cabin. 'I started down the slope and was really getting into the rhythm. There's nothing like a long ski run,' he smiled.

'But then...?' Alisa prompted him. She'd suspected there was something more to this story that had come to Dr. A's mind. As middle child, she was used to prompting and encouraging.

Will gazed at the one dark-haired child between the two redheads. 'But then, the earth parted.' His eyes were level but his lips thinned straight across. It was a grim memory.

'A crevasse?' Kathi guessed, breathless.

'A crevasse,' Will nodded, deliberately lifting his chin to answer truthfully, but keeping most of horror out of this story for the children. 'Not that I saw it. The way was smooth in front of me, and the next thing I knew I was hanging upside down, with my feet threatening to come out of the bindings over about seventy-five to a hundred feet of drop that I could see in the reflected moonlight. Who knew how much deeper it was beyond that, not that it would matter very much.'

'Oh,' breathed Ted, his dark pupils dilated. He was so sleepy from a happy day on the mountainside, but Dr. Asbury's story was too exciting for him to be willing to give up and curl on the other sofa with me.

'My skis were straddling the long narrow gap. The tips had caught on one side and the heel edge on the other. The tips might hold. There was just enough of a curl up so there was something to dig in. But I worried about the back end. My skis were flat from the heel of my boot all the way back. The edge was just lying there on the snow, with nothing to keep it there. I knew it could slide any minute.'

'I'd have screamed,' Alisa exhaled.

'No, no, you wouldn't have,' Kathi said thoughtfully. 'If the Germans or the Italians knew you were there, they'd come after you and shoot you.'

'Or stand there laughing a while and then kick the end of the ski loose,' Will said low.

'And let you fall?' Alisa cried.

'Save ammunition,' Will explained, shrugging. He knew he was getting in too deep here. There are realities to war that children don't need to know yet. Deliberately, he hitched forward in the sofa and sat up, his hands raised to demonstrate. 'See, my problem was that I was suspended upside-down. The bindings on the skis were made to hold me the other way. I wasn't sure how long they would hold my weight opposite of what they were made for.'

'Were you scared?' Ted asked.

'Uh, yeah, I was scared. And cold. And not sure from one second to the next that I'd have much to say about what would happen. But after the initial terrifying moments, I knew I'd better do something. Nothing looked likely to get better by just hanging there.'

'What could you do?' Alisa asked.

'You needed to get up, but, oh, that's tough, bending in the middle and getting your hands up to reach the skis,' Kathi said, frowning. 'Unless you could reach the wall of the crevasse and work your hands up punching into the snow higher and higher.'

'Good idea, Kathi,' Will approved. 'I didn't do that, but it might have worked. The trouble was I was afraid of every pull and tug on the skis, afraid I would jar them loose. When I shrugged out of that backpack, I could hear it fall what seemed like a long, long time before I hear it hit.'

'Oh,' Alisa whispered.

'You could bend in the middle and reach straight up to the skis?' Kathi asked. 'Wow!'

'Army training makes you something of an athlete whether you want to be or not,' Will grinned. 'Training plus adrenaline. Yes, I reached up as though I was reaching for Heaven. It was the third try, and I knew after that one I didn't have enough strength to go up directly. I crunched those abdominal muscles like they'd never been used before, and, yes, I touched those skis. Nothing had ever felt so good to my fingertips as that pliant wood. Ah!' Will leaned back into the sofa cushions with a huge grin and sigh.

Alisa and Kathi were staring at him wide-eyed, but Ted nodded. His eyes closed and he swayed. Alisa drew him toward her shoulder while Kathi puffed up pillows and piled them so they could lay him against them with as little disturbance as possible.

'Okay,' Kathi said once they'd settled their little brother, 'so you could touch the skis, but your feet were still in those bindings and the skis were still not anchored to anything.'

'Oh, it was touchy all right,' Will said. 'Every second I expected the whole rig to let loose and tumble down into the deep cold. I was sweating, despite the snow. And the wind that was starting up. What an eerie moaning howl that gave. Have you ever blown across the top of an empty pop bottle? It was a little like that only fainter. And more unearthly.'

When Will shuddered, the girls did, too. I thought one or the other would scoot across the braided rug to my lap, but neither wanted to get that far from the storyteller.

Will sat a few minutes gazing into the fire behind the grill of his pot-bellied stove.

'Well, those fingertips told me I had a chance to stay alive,' he took up his story again after a few minutes. 'I worked my hand up to grip the one ski and just hung there a while, breathing hard and not knowing whether to laugh or cry. The angle of my ankles in the boots was odd, and that seemed to help my get first one foot out and then the other while I hung there by the other hand. I'd had to drop my mitten to be able to work at the boots

- somehow I didn't dare fuss with the bindings as I was afraid the skis would be sure to jar loose - and that hand was getting mighty cold.

'It's funny, then I began to worry about how cold my feet would get walking in the snow without boots. Maybe it helped to have my mind wander a little, worrying about the next steps instead of what could happen during the one I was on. Anyway, as I was loosening the boots, I managed to get my arm up and over the ski so I was hanging by my elbow. That felt safer. And just as my feet tumbled out of the boots, I got myself hitched up to my armpit on the ski. As the boots loosened I grabbed for the other ski with my free hand and let gravity do what it would. I was praying it would only straighten me out and not take me with it.

'What a relief it was to have my feet underneath me!' Will laid his head back against the cushions and gazed at the wood planks of the ceiling. His mouth opened and then partially closed in an 'Oh,' but we didn't hear any sound.

We waited.

With a grin, Will sat up and looked at the girls. 'The rest was comparatively easy. I inched my way along the skis, praying they would hold, and when I got to the side, I hiked my self up and out of there.'

Kathi frowned again. 'The snow edge was that solid?'

Smiling, Will turned my oldest and shook his head slowly. 'Well, not exactly. It took some maneuvering at the front edge of the ski but eventually I worked my way to where the snow was hard packed enough to hold me, though there was a moment there when I finally got up onto my knees and the whole snowpack underneath me threatened to let go,' he said.

Ted woke with a start. 'What?'

'It's okay, Tedder, Dr. A was just telling us how he fell into the big hole while he was skiing,' Alisa told him.

'Oh, yeah,' Ted said, sitting up and rubbing his eyes. He stared at Will. 'Did you get out?'

SADIE

'My kids are going to hunt elk,' Sadie chirped, nodding her head so the gray bangs hula-ed.

The kindly older woman beside her on the bus seat smiled politely. 'No one in my family hunts except with a camera,' she murmured. She turned to glance out the window at the passing Beaverton storefronts.

'And I'm going with them,' Sadie announced, triumphant.

The seatmate twisted to face her. 'Oh?'

'Oh, yes! I go every year that I can. These last couple years my son Johnny has such a high truck - you know, raised up over the wheels, though dear knows why. Well, with my arthritis, I can barely climb up inside that steel and chrome monster of his. So,' Sadie giggled, 'last year my Johnny got behind me, I thought to give me a boost. And what do you know, instead of a shimmy, he picked me up like a little girl and lifted me up into the front seat. We laughed some over that, the whole camp, I'll tell ya. Uh oh, here's my stop coming up. Gotta get off. It's been sure nice talking with you. Hope we catch the same bus again soon.'

Sadie hustled to the stairwell at the street side door half way to the back of the bus. She turned to wave as the Tri-Met swung in beside an illegally parked car next to the curb and the door folded open with a whoosh.

'Happy hunting!' Sadie called back, and her seatmate smiled and waved in return.

No one knows exactly what happened next.

The bus driver swears Sadie was clear before he pulled away.

The driver of the car in the bus stop zone is sure he'd started out of the way before the bus pulled in. He'd only stopped for a minute to run in and pick up his drycleaning and he saw the bus coming. So he would take an oath that it was the bus driver's fault for not letting him get out of the no parking area and clear the stop for a passenger to disembark safely.

Sadie remembers stepping off the lower stair and then waking up groggy and very sore in the hospital. Daughter-in-law Suzette was holding her hand.

'Johnny, she's awake,' Sue hissed at her husband asleep in the chair in the corner of the room. 'Johnny!'

John tilted forward with a bang of the front legs on the floor.

'My boy's been tilting his chair back again, hasn't he?' Sadie laughed. 'That trick of his has gotten him in so many spills, I can't remember.' But Sadie's speech was more garbled than she realized.

'Now, Mom, take it easy,' John told her, drawing his chair beside the bed and taking her hand. His own words were slurred a little with fatigue.

'You're only just out of surgery, Momma S.,' Sue told her.

'Surgery?' Sadie's eyes opened wide.

'Your hip,' John explained, a lot more awake by this time. 'It was pretty well crushed in the accident. They were a long time putting you back together.'

'Accident? Oh, when I got off that bus...' But try as she might, Sadie could not remember anything beyond the friendly wave of the woman who liked hunting only with a camera.

'Sleep now, Momma S. Get some good sleep and we can talk more about it later when you feel better.'

It sounded like a good plan, but of course it didn't quite work out that way.

The next week was filled with pain that Sadie could not control, even with medication.

Elk season came and went. Sadie was asked to push through much of the discomfort as the physical therapists guided her self-torture in hopes of returning as much function to her battered body as possible. Sadie gritted her teeth and continued to work through discouragement and hurt.

'I'm going hunting again,' she told herself, dreaming of the open ground where the family sometimes left her in the camp. In her mind she heard the haunting calls of the sociable California quails. She felt the sun baking one shoulder while the other, in shadow, remained chilled, and she loved the sensation enough to keep from moving. She sniffed as though she could draw in the hot buttered popcorn smell of sun beating on honeysuckle. In a moment of rest, Sadie closed her eyes and traded stares with a mangy coyote that had sensed her presence and refused to move until she had proved she meant him no harm. Or until he forgot where she was, more likely, Sadie chuckled to herself. Deer did that, too. If you stayed still long enough they lost track of you. One or two might stay wary, but most of the rest would go back to their grazing.

How awesome it was to sit quietly in the midst of the busy-ness of Nature.

'I'm going hunting again, even if this time it's only with a camera,' Sadie vowed.

And she did.

It was deer season - almost a year since that step off into the agonizing void. But Sadie was out of the cast, though still barely able to move on her own. She struggled with the walker that made her feel so much older than she knew herself to be inside.

'You know how rugged the ground is, Mom,' John reasoned. 'Here you are just about making it on level ground in your own back yard, and you want to go with us into the woods? You'll never be able to get around even with the walker with the paths so rough. And if you fall again...'

Sadie looked up at him, square in the eyes. 'I'm going,' she said quietly, and at last he frowned, lifted his broad shoulders in a huge sigh, and nodded.

Sadie grinned. 'Yea,' she said, under her breath.

'Oh, boy,' she whispered when John's pickup bounced to a halt in the clearing that was to be their campsite.

Aline, Dale and Suzette had gotten there first and already had two of the tents up and the rocks circled for their cooking fire. They rose and waved.

'Hi, Mom! Hi, Johnny! Come on over for a mug of hot coffee. How did you stand the jouncing on the logging road, Mom? I knew we should have had you shipped in by helicopter.'

'And where would it have landed?' Sadie asked. 'Those pilots are good, but you'd have had to take down at least one of those tents to give him room.'

'And the downwash from the chopper would probably have knocked down the other,' Dale chuckled. 'Maybe even a couple of the trees.'

Sadie grinned and accepted the coffee, black and strong, the way she liked it. She closed her mouth and protested no more, both because she'd made her point, and because she was more tired from the truck trip than she ever hoped to admit to her family.

Exhausted, Sadie slept like a log in the cot Johnny made up for her in the camper hutch in the bed of the pickup.

The next morning, as Aline and Sue made breakfast, Sadie stirred but found it worth all of her pride to move around without groaning aloud. The hip hurt worse than she had dreamed that it would. But if she wasn't to spoil the hunting for her children, she had to bite her lip and get herself ready without a sound.

'What's that on your lip, Mom?' Aline asked when Sadie signaled that she was ready to join them for the hot cakes and tumbled eggs.

'Dratted mosquitoes,' Sadie muttered. John and Dale nodded agreement while Aline peered at her mother, but said nothing.

As the girls gathered the dishes, Aline, with her back turned, said, 'I think I'll stay here in camp today.'

'You turn around this minute and look at me,' Sadie ordered.

Surprised by the sharpness in her tone, Aline turned.

'Now listen here, young lady,' Sadie sputtered, 'you are going out with Dale and that's all there is to it. You came on this trip to hunt, and hunt you will. You hear me?'

'But, Mom...' Aline started.

'No buts,' Sadie ordered. Aline had to laugh.

'You make me feel like a little girl in pigtails.'

'And if you stay in camp I know it will be to baby-sit me. I'm too young to be that old, and it was a broken hip, that's all. I'm not an invalid.'

Dale had come up to stand behind Aline. Johnny came to the edge of the cook circle and halted with the load of wood in his arms. Sue rose from beside the fire and peered at her husband.

Slowly Sadie shifted on the walker to glare at each of them in turn.

'Remember the year you left me in the cab of the truck?'

Johnny nodded as he lowered the wood. 'We left it in first gear so you could take off the brake and move when you wanted to.'

'And I did, thank you very much. I was self-sufficient before I had you two, and I'm self-sufficient now,' she grinned, 'within reason.'

Son-in-law Dale smiled that patient smile and shook his head. Sue and Aline looked at each other and grinned. She'd won again. It was so important to Sadie to be independent. If she ever got to the point where she let them baby her, they knew that that would be the beginning of the end.

Johnny gouged at the stump she'd pointed out to him, smoothing its top and hacking it to conform a little more to her derrière. He and Dale helped her into the eider down sleeping bag as Aline and Sue drew it up around her and settled her in. They left supplies at hand and stood back, eyebrows lifted. 'Are you sure?'

'I like it better here than in the truck. I can hear the birds and a lot more animals will come close to me here than will approach the truck even when I'm still. You got enough stuff here for me to rest easy for a week. So go, already.'

Sadie waved them away, lifted her face for the kiss from each of them and waved again as each couple took up their rifles and disappeared among the trees. She listened a long time to be sure they weren't circling back to spy on her before she let out the low moan she'd been swallowing.

'Well, of course, it hurts, lady,' she told herself. 'What did you expect when you get crushed against a moving bus - or whatever did happen? I guess we'll never know for sure. But you're alive. You've been given a bonus few years to watch the grandchildren and the great grandchildren. To hear the chirps and caws and screeches of your birds. To maybe see a critter or two steal across your line of sight.

'You're a lucky lady, Sadie. Always have been. But incredibly lucky to be given one more chance to hunt.'

SELMA ❄

The huge-shouldered, muscular Swedish loggers quailed and turned to Selma. They'd faced snakes and bears and cougars in the woods, sometimes even fought them one-on-one. And they'd seen blood before. Horrific injuries happened to timbermen, what with the accidents that will happen any time men are wielding heavy iron tools with sharp-honed edges. Or timber falling sometimes off true in soft ground. Or a rotten spar tree slabbing out and splitting a high-climber's lifeline, bringing him down with the tree he has been climbing to the ground. Or, more frequently if only because there are so many cables and so many men doing complex tasks in close proximity to them, a "line" looping or taking up slack or flipping under tension and whipping out to deliver a man a slicing or a crushing blow. Oh, the loggers knew blood, all right, but they came back out to the woods day after day, knowing full well that one of them could be maimed for life, or killed, with no more notice than an instant of singing metal.

But a woman in labor? That was different. "Selma!" they'd cry, and the determined little blond lady with the snapping blue eyes would come in and take over.

She seldom went out to the logging camps except for the birth of a first-generation Swede. Her husband, Mr. Nash, worked in a small town in northern Minnesota, where Selma had a flourishing clientele. Even local doctors respected her skill in handling complications, her cool head in an emergency, her natural leadership in getting panicked family members to do what was needed.

Selma herself gave the credit to God. With no children of her own, Selma was still an active member of her Sunday services and teaching programs. The money she earned as a midwife was meted out in (then huge) $5.00 sums to charitable organizations. Selma's brother Alfred was disgusted with her for wasting all the money.

Selma had come to the United States before the turn of the twentieth century as a nanny and maid for a family emigrating from Sweden. Alfred had gotten permission to come to work in America because he had a sister already here, so he really couldn't say much to her about her money or anything else. But he did bluster some from the far Pacific Northwest when she bought a tract of land in the uncivilized interior of central California.

"That's a big piece of nothing!" he tried to tell her.

"It's not nothing; I bought it from a clergyman," she replied, cleaning up after delivering Alfred's second child, his first son. She'd traveled all the way from Minnesota to Oregon to be there for him and she didn't appreciate his tone of exasperation. He had such a prejudice against ministers. "A clergyman wouldn't lie about how valuable that land is."

Alfred rolled his eyes but knew better than to push his sister any further. Her small fists were resting on her hips as she looked up at him. Besides, little Manfred was crying. He'd been crying since he was born. Maybe that continuing noise was what was putting them both on edge.

Manfred continued to cry until finally Selma let him suckle a taste of whiskey. And then the baby slept - for days.

Selma held that plot of California timberland for years, perhaps afraid to try to sell it for fear that Alfred had been right - at least until the timber grew. Late in life, when her blond hair had turned to silver and then to white, she let Alfred handle the logging of the timber and then the sale of the land to a plywood company. Alfred secured far more money for her than she'd ever dreamed and both smiled smugly, sure they'd been right. Fortunately they'd tacitly agreed it was a subject not to be discussed.

Selma was in her sixties now, and knew there wasn't a whole lot longer that even she could brave the rigors of another cross-country trip to see her brother. Alfred by now had three young Nordgrens: tall, slender Alfhild, big-boned, personable Fred, and blond, teenage high-climber Earl. Both boys were busy logging with their father in their woods during much of her few days' visit, but Earl was able to join the family driving Selma to the railroad depot in Portland to see her off.

Earl was a delightful audience. He grinned slowly, but his eyes twinkled as she told them of her adventure with the fire.

"Your whole house, Aunt Selma?"

"Every eave and nook and cranny," she said, wiping her hands on her skirt. It had happened almost a decade before, but Selma could still feel the sweat on her palms and the desperation and then the determination. "My whole house. Everything I'd built or sewn or Mr. Nash had carved for me or sweated to buy me. Everything. All of it in flames that were dancing from every window and rising higher than the roofline."

"You must have been so frightened," Alfhild gasped.

"I was mad," Selma stated and Alfhild peered at her, eyes wide. "I'd fought through so many times - made babies breathe when everybody had already given up on them, when they were so blue, you could have lost them against the sky. Brought mothers through when they were bleeding so much there wasn't a whisper of a prayer for them. So I wasn't about to just stand there and watch everything we had in the world go up in smoke."

"So what did you do?" Alfhild asked, almost afraid to hear the answer.

"I got myself in there," Selma told her, lips tight.

"Into the flames?"

Selma only nodded, but she could see that Earl would probably been right behind her on her dash across the lawn and up onto the porch. He had that Nordgren stubborn streak, too.

"Did you rescue anything?" Alfred asked, ever the practical one.

"Well, yes, and no."

Earl glanced at Aunt Selma, then shut his mouth.

But Alfred had to push on. "You did get something out of the fire, then? What was it?"

"Boots," she admitted finally.

"You risked your life in a raging fire to rescue a pair of boots?"

"Who said they were a pair?"

Her brother and sister-in-law and niece gaped at her. Only young Earl smiled at the irony of life.

"I was dead set against that fire getting everything I owned. I snatched up what I could find. So what if those boots didn't match?"

BEGGIN' STRIP

They'd sailed back to Sweden after the amputation. After many months of rehabilitation, they decided it was the perfect time to go back to the land of their birth and youth. Back to loving family they hadn't seen in so long.

Hildur rolled her eyes, and Alfred smiled at the eager face of his nephew Per. Hildur had already told him that she was "fed up" with this visit to homeland Sweden. She'd only meant that uncles and cousins and now younger brother Lars had feted them, feasted them, treated them like royalty on their visit to this hospitable country.

But little Per was such a bright youngster. He really wanted to know about America. What could Alfred do but continue the stories of his adventures in the Pacific Northwest?

'Auntie Hildur says you had one crew start on one side of the mountain and another crew on the other and they tunneled so well they were only off a foot when they met,' Per exclaimed. 'Is that right, Uncle Alfred? Are you such a good engineer, then?'

'Ah, young Per, you will learn in your life that when wives talk about you, they will either nag or brag,' Alfred said solemnly and Lars chuckled.

'Why did you give up the railroad tunnel building, then, brother?' Lars asked.

'Crooks they were. My tunnels I build right or not at all,' Alfred half-rose in his chair, but Hildur was shaking her head with a frown. If he got started on that, he and Lars would be hours comparing the bad deeds of greedy men in both their countries. And his gentle-souled wife had nursed him too long and too faithfully after the accident for him to ignore her needs now. She was so tired; she wanted to go home.

Alfred glanced at Hildur to reassure her, then settled into his overstuffed chair in his younger brother's front room. He smiled at young Per.

'I wanted land of our own, you see. I wanted a homestead where we could have cows and chickens and a big garden that means we depend on no one but ourselves. The land we found was in Oregon. Not so good land for farming. It is on a hill. But there is good water and the trees grow tall. We can walk under them for hours and only seldom see the sun. The Great Depression came and we were glad to have our garden and our own milk and eggs.

'We learned to cut the trees to sell firewood. And then my boys - they are both big, strapping young men now - my sons learned with me to fell trees for lumber. Earl was not a lot bigger than you are now when he began to high climb. 100, 120, 150 foot trees, he would cut off the limbs as he climbed up, and then at 80 or 100 feet, wherever we needed the spar tree to be tall, there he would stop and cut off the rest of the tree above him.'

'Are Earl and Manfred running your logging company now?' Lars asked.

Alfred glanced at Hildur. They were. The sons were doing what the father could not. There was sympathy in his beloved's eyes. And resignation. And pride, knowing what he had been through and what he had conquered.

'Tell me about them, please, Uncle Alfred,' Per begged. 'It is good to be so strong and able in the woods.'

'It is good, young Per. But it is hard work. And dangerous. Why, only this year ago, Earl was trying to sand the donkey engine so it would haul the logs without slipping. The huge crank arm whipped back on him without warning, grazing his head and tearing off all his clothes. He was many minutes before he could wake up. Even Early.' Alfred closed his eyes, remembering.

He'd been terrified, thinking his youngest son was dead, lying there still and white. Earl had awakened, finally, but for the first time in years wasn't able to carry on with the work. Even when his wrists had just been pinned back and smashed, Earl had climbed that afternoon because his father needed something done. But this time, Earl was head sick, not just in pain. Alfred had had to send him home.

And then it happened. Alfred himself had tried to sand that stubborn donkey engine. His pant leg caught in the gears and before Manfred could stop the machine, Alfred's foot was dragged in and crushed. It was the way things were in the woods. You didn't moan and groan about it. But the weeks of pain at home, and then the gangrene and the needed amputation of his leg. And then the healing. It had taken all of Hildur's love and support to get him to strap on the wooden leg. But here he was, walking again. With more of a limp than he wanted the world to see, but walking. And when they went home to America, Alfred was going back into the woods to work. He'd show them.

When he opened his eyes, Hildur and Lars were staring at him with concern.

A Swede hates pity. Alfred heaved up from the chair.

'Why don't you men go for a walk?' Hildur suggested. 'We women have important things to gossip about and you are only in our way.'

Lars chuckled aloud. 'Come, brother, if you are up to it?'

'Just try to keep up,' Alfred growled. But he glanced at his Hildur. She'd saved his pride again. And to think he'd nearly married her sister - prettier, but not nearly so down to earth.

Per jumped up to follow them. After a few blocks he was running ahead. The men talked of politics and the corruption that follows greed. They only realized the approach of the shabby beggar when Per returned to walk close at his father's hip.

'Sirs, could you help a poor man?' the beggar wheedled. 'I can't work, you see?' He raised his mutilated thumb in their faces with a pathetic smile on his face.

Grimacing, Lars stepped back and his hand went to the coins in his pocket.

But Alfred bent forward, hiking up his trouser leg. 'Why don't you pay me?' he asked reasonably as he displayed the wooden leg.

The beggar stared, then turned and ran.

Per gaped at the wood, and then, as his uncle lowered the pant leg, at Alfred's face.

'There's more danger than glamour in a man's life, boy. But it's almost worth it to see a fellow like that run away.'

FOOTLESS IN SPOKANE

Alone, thousands of miles from home and family and friends, Swede curled on his side in the cot, not believing the gripping pain in his belly.

In his native Sweden, he'd had never had a sick day in his life. In the Pacific Northwest of this America he had emigrated to, he thrived on the hardships and hard work with the railroad. And he was learning - surveying, engineering, everything he could from peering over the shoulders of the men who were planning and building. Some of these educated men of the turn of the twentieth century had frowned at his persistence. A few applauded his keen wonder to know and took time to explain.

Always he'd been strong to help them so they would be inclined to teach him more.

And then the pain came, unnerving him the more because he couldn't stand up to it. For the first time, he took to his bed in the cold tent. Funny, how when you're working up a sweat, you never notice the cold. But now that he'd been felled like one of the tall pines, the cold gnawed at his shoulders, his back, his toes, though his middle simmered in a growing fire. Shifting, Swede tucked his hands low against his abdomen as though he could brace himself against the hurt. Opening his eyes after one biting wave of agony, he saw that snow had drifted through the tent flap fidgeting in the wind. White and crystalline, it piled in a long triangle on the plank floor beside him. It wasn't melting.

'Lord help the poor slob caught out in chill like this,' Swede thought.

And then the pain swept over him in a flood so intense that he cried out, no longer caring about wind or cold or anyone else. Swede was drowning in his own writhing world.

At the tracks, conditions worsened until finally even the boss had to concede they couldn't make headway in weather like this. Cussing under his breath, he sent the men back to their flimsy shelters. Giant Olaf was the first to enter the tent shared with Swede and two others.

'Yo, Swede, you saved yourself a bit of frostbite with your belly-aching this day,' Olaf growled cheerfully and clapped his huge hand on Swede's shoulder.

At his cry, Olaf bent over and hauled his tightly curled friend toward him so he could study his face.

'Per,' the huge man ordered, 'tell the boss man we are hitching up a wagon and taking Swede here to see a doctor.'

'But there's nothing much between here and Spokane,' Per protested.

'I would not care if there was nothing much between here and Oslo! We go!'

The small town doctor eleven miles away in that storm stood up from examining Swede and looked up to meet Olaf's eyes.

'So, you know what is wrong with Swede here?'

'Appendicitis,' the doctor answered, then turned away to dip his hands in the porcelain bowl.

'Appen...' Olaf stumbled over the foreign word.

'A little tube on the large intestine - the guts. It's infected. I think it's burst.' The old man shrugged sloping shoulders.

'So what you do?'

'I do nothing. Anything I would do would kill him. But there are doctors in Spokane who might be able to operate. Take the appendix out with a knife.'

'Cut open his belly?'

The old man nodded and shrugged again. 'If he survives to get to Spokane. Terrible weather.'

Per looked up at Olaf.

'Yah, we go,' Olaf said and bent to pick up Swede as though he were a babe.

'So you survived?' Dr. Greystone smiled. 'I knew when your frozen pals carted you in that you were a tough one. So we went ahead with the surgery. I think it turned out well,' the surgeon said with no false modesty.

It was the first time Swede had seen the long, scabbed line low on his abdomen.

'How does it feel?'

Swede took a breath. It hurt even to do that, but when the doctor finished with the bandage, he hitched himself up nearly to sitting against the iron bedstead.

'Tomorrow I walk.'

'No, no, that's much too soon,' the doctor said. 'Maybe three days from now, we can help you stand up, but even that would be early. Our new mothers aren't allowed out of their beds for a week.'

'Tomorrow I walk,' Swede told him.

Dr. Greystone stared into his eyes. 'We'll see tomorrow,' he said without protesting further.

'He's one tough Swede from the Old Country. You couldn't have stopped him,' Greystone told the frustrated nurses as they hovered over their surgery patient swaying on his feet beside his bed the next morning. 'In the meantime, can you do something to hush the pair of peacocks there at the far end of the ward? Their constant complaints are disturbing my surgery patients who need their sleep. Those two are screeching more over hangnails than this Swede over an open belly.'

'Dr. Greystone?' a little nurse cried as she hurried in pointing behind her to two burly policemen carrying a pale, gaunt man between them. 'You will never believe this!'

It was unbelievable that a man in that condition was apparently still alive.

'Get into your bed now. I'm going to need these nurses of yours,' Greystone ordered the Swede, who responded more quickly than he could have willed himself to do under other circumstances.

'Put him in here,' the surgeon pointed to the bed next to the Swede and stripped off the top cover so the policemen could lay him out. As the little nurse covered the patient with clean linen Greystone started. There was no lump where the feet should stick up.

'Accidental amputation?' Greystone demanded as he bent forward to set his stethoscope at the patient's chest.

'Not accidental, Doctor,' the taller of the two large policemen said. 'Done it himself.'

Greystone lifted the earpiece away. 'What?'

'A gold miner up in the hills. Frostbite going into gangrene, evidently. Says he knew it'd creep up his legs and kill him, so he cut off his own feet with his knife and crawled miles to a railroad camp. They brung him in.'

Greystone whistled and turned to the Swede. 'Is this guy some cousin of yours from Stockholm?' he said with admiration. 'This one's got to be Swedish, too.'

139

BRIDGE TO THE FUTURE

'I may have lost my leg, but I haven't lost my senses!' Alfred snapped and both his logger sons lowered their eyes.

What could they tell him? Earl had been to the corner of the property less than a month ago. He knew where it was - could almost tramp there blindfolded. Fred was the strong one, but he had a lot of other interests and didn't pay close attention to details like boundaries the way Earl did. But there was no doubt he too could have found the corner of their logging property after a short search. At least he had pointed in the right direction.

Pa, on the other hand, was just plain wrong. Only he wouldn't listen to either of them.

'I'll find it myself,' he stormed, lifted that shoe fastened to the end of his wooden leg and stomped off.

He'd hated having to use an artificial limb - hated to admit that he was a cripple. But once he made the decision and strapped it on for the first time, he realized that when he pulled the pant leg down, no one would know if he didn't tell them. So he learned to walk with as little a limp as he could get away with. And he never said anything, or asked for special favors. He was determined not to ask for help.

But tramping in the woods is not the same as strolling on a sidewalk. The ground is uneven. Weeds and leaves disguise potholes that you don't recognize until you step in them. And then it is a matter of catching your balance. Or falling.

Alfred had fallen any number of times these past weeks. But he never let his sons help him up.

'Like a baby,' he'd mutter, disgusted with himself. And, like a toddler, he'd pick himself up and readjust the shoe and head off again, grimacing.

'What are we gonna do, Fred?' Earl asked when their father was nearly out of sight in the wrong direction.

'We tried to tell him,' Fred shrugged. 'You gonna traipse after him? Think he'll be grateful? Come on, we've got our own work to do.'

The "boys," now in their twenties, went back to the spar tree.

'Besides,' Fred said as though Earl had protested, 'we've been running this whole operation on our own while Pa was in the hospital. You'd think he'd give us credit for knowing a little bit about what we're doing.'

'Still, he's not that good on that leg yet. And there's a lot of felled logs down that way that he'll have to scramble over.'

'Best if we let him just come back on his own. He'll holler if he gets into trouble.'

But that was just it. Would he? Earl shook his head, but leaned in to help his older brother attach the chain to hook the log to the skyline. He'd just have to keep an ear open and listen carefully, he guessed. What more could they do? Trying to follow after their father would insult him, and Alfred was a proud, resourceful man. Earl had no desire to take anything away from his father's sense of manhood.

But Alfred didn't come back. Earl lifted his hard hat and wiped a sweaty arm across his forehead. He helped guide the last of the logs down as Fred maneuvered it with the donkey engine. Earl scrambled up to unhook the chain, then climbed down to meet his brother walking toward him. He could see that even Fred was concerned.

'It's been too long,' Earl put their worry into words.

'He'll hate to admit he was wrong. And he'll hate having us rescue him.'

'But by this time, I'm afraid he does need rescuing. I just hope he isn't hurt again.'

'Yeah,' Fred muttered. 'You figure where he went?'

'Pretty much, I guess,' Earl nodded. Their property included more than a thousand acres of wooded hillsides at the eastern edge of the Oregon Coastal range, and Earl knew every foot of it. 'There's some gullies that way.' He said no more. Fred knew as well as he did what that could mean.

Their trees were tall and dense enough to block any view of the Cascade Mountain snow peaks behind them. The air hung chilly even now in mid-afternoon this late in the fall. Neither son wore a jacket. They worked up too much a sweat while lumberjacking that they didn't need to wrap up while they were working, usually even in winter. But Earl flung his wool sweater over his shoulder when they started out. And Fred did the same without a word.

They searched about a hundred yards apart, close enough to hear each other yell if they found him but covering more territory than they could have staying together. They were almost systematic, in case they had to come back and comb the area again. Neither son would admit it, but their father had been gone long enough that they couldn't count on his being able to holler to them for help.

They whacked large stands of brush with switches, just in case. What startled away made them catch their breath once in a while, but there was no sign of Alfred.

'Yo!' Fred hollered. As Earl came scrambling toward him, he picked up and held out the shoe from the base of Alfred's wooden leg. It was crusted with mud and leaves. 'You were right. He came this way. I'd seen some blundering marks in the moss on a couple fallen logs, but that could have been bear. But this...'

'He was so sure he knew,' Earl nodded. 'There's a ravine just up ahead,' he said, shuddering. He moved back, widening the distance between them as he continued the search with his breath held now.

Finally, they both emerged into comparative open. Fred looked across at Earl at the crest of the ravine.

'Pa!' Fred bellowed.

'Listen!'

And there it was, a faint cry from the bottom. The young men couldn't see him, but they knew their father was down there.

It took them only minutes to get to him. Alfred was shaken and angry and covered with mud and leaves much as his shoe had been. The hinge between the wooden leg and foot was jammed with debris and Alfred swore as he tried to pry the stuff loose. His face was pale with deep pink blotches in the hollows of his cheeks. His lips were pursed and his jaw set.

He hated to let them help him but was too tired to protest. Earl knew where there was a gentler slope than the one they had tumbled down. He led them along the bottom of the ravine for a while and pointed up. How he wished he'd had the foresight to bring a rope.

'Oofdah,' Alfred muttered and Earl smiled grimly at the all-encompassing Swedish exclamation. They started up.

At first Alfred shook off their hands from his arm. But soon the slope steepened and he lifted his cane for one son or the other to pull on. Sweating and pale and rasping for breath, Alfred made it on his own one foot and wooden leg. But he was exhausted before they reached the top.

He wouldn't quit. He wouldn't hear of them trying to pack him up on Fred's back. He only gripped that cane fiercely and grunted for Fred to pull. Near the top he was too done in to say anything when Earl braced and then shoved him from behind.

143

At the top, Alfred let himself down to sit against the base of a tree. Earl dropped his sweater over his father's shoulders and stepped away so Alfred wouldn't have to protest. It was only when he looked back at his father's stooped shoulders that he realized the man was too exhausted even to try.

Earl ripped the bark off of a section of branch, one piece at a time. How were they going to explain their father's condition to their mother? She'd been through so much with him, first with the crushed foot and then the infection and the amputation. Alfred was not a patient patient. And then his depression until he finally accepted the fact of his loss and stood up to it. Literally.

She'd told them to watch out for him in the woods, that he might be trying more than he was ready to accomplish.

But she'd know how difficult he was to dissuade. She'd understand, eventually.

She did. She nursed him yet again. And when he was ready, she stood back and let him go out again with his sons into his woods.

If he'd had a calk (pronounced 'cork') shoe on that wooden foot, it would have been different. But the shoe was nearly smooth-soled.

The old tree that had fallen across the gully was a good hundred and twenty feet long. It was thick and sturdy and well secured at the other end so ordinarily it would have been like walking across a hundred-foot bridge. Granted, there were no handrails, but Earl and Fred and Alfred had crossed much wobblier spans. They'd crossed even deeper gullies rather than climb all the way down and all the way back up the other side.

This gully was maybe ninety feet deep. And Alfred's shoe was not fitted with the cleats that give a logger traction against bark.

He was tired. He'd insisted on coming out with his boys, but he still couldn't keep up with them the way he wanted to, even though they did all the actual work and he only 'supervised.'

Fred had marched across with scarcely a look down. He set off into the woods on the other side without looking back.

Earl, also carrying gear, lumbered across, but stood at the far end now, peering back at his father. Alfred climbed up onto the huge end and started forward.

And then he stopped. A third of the way across, suddenly he was frozen with doubt and fear such as he'd seldom known. He was shaking. Actually shaking. His knees trembled and threatened to give way under his weight. His hand clutched the end of his cane, barely holding his balance.

Those shoes! If only...

Earl set down most of his gear and was stepping toward his end of the log bridge.

Alfred glared across the log at his youngest as though he were to blame.

'I'm so afraid...' Alfred murmured. And then he screwed his eyes shut and opened them deliberately, inhaled until his chest was filled and he could take in no more. He blew out the air and set his jaw.

There was no boast. No wild cry of defiance. Alfred simply stepped forward after a single look down to the depths below him.

He walked across that bridge.

He was scowling, but his eyes were bright.

Alfred hitched himself off the end of the log and strode past his son, now smiling at him with pride.

SMOKIN' CRADLE

La Wanda's birth gave new meaning to the term, "cloudy future." In fact, there were moments when her family wasn't at all sure there was a future - for any of them.

Vernonia is a pretty town set in towering, Pacific Northwest forest. In 1933 there were many trees which, when felled, could accommodate a six-foot man lying across its stump without having his feet hang over. There were vast stretches of timber so tall and dense that they shut out the sun. La Wanda's grandparents knew trails where you could start in at one edge of a canopy acres in any direction, and never see the sky until you hiked to the other edge. The trees gave shade and protection and a calm born of a sense of timelessness.

The trees also gave timber, and logging gave the livelihood to ninety per cent of the little sawmill town of Vernonia, nearly half way between Portland and the mouth of the Columbia River.

But trees burn.

In the late summer of 1933 the trees of northwest Oregon burned with a vengeance. It was the first in a series of huge forest fires that gained the name "Tillamook Burn."

Near drought conditions had left the woods dry as tinder. At Glenwood, only a couple dozen miles from Vernonia, friction of log pulled over log caused the dry bark to ignite. It was an oversized example of what Boy Scouts try to do with two dry sticks when no one has a match. The fire that resulted from this accidental conflagration was soon so oversized that square miles of standing timber quickly added to the flames.

The smoke was so dense for weeks that even Portlanders drove with their lights on in the daytime.

When that inferno was less than a week old, La Wanda decided to enter the world.

Desperate, the family sent word to the doctor, but there was no way he could come, so La Wanda's grandparents looked at each other across the gloom of the sooty room and rolled up their sleeves. Coughing, they delivered the lusty little girl.

But a baby's first breath taken in a smoky room leads to coughing and choking.

'We've got to do something!' Grandpa cried. 'She can hardly breathe!' He searched and found a cardboard box not much bigger than a shoebox.

Grandma cocked her head, then broke into a closed-mouthed smile. 'I've got cheesecloth,' she said. Fumbling through her dry goods, she brought out the remnants of a bolt of loose-woven cotton mesh.

Grandpa took a long section from her and went to wet it down. Grandma wrapped the new baby in crib blankets and laid her in the cardboard box. Grandpa covered the open top with the wet cheesecloth and they knelt to stuff the box under the bed. That was as much protection as they could give the newborn from the sooty air.

They watched and waited. Gradually the infant's gagging cries diminished. Grandma clutched her husband's hand. Could tiny La Wanda breathe in there?

He held her until the baby went still. Together they lifted the cheesecloth. La Wanda lay breathing regularly, contented and asleep.

'Ah, sweet Lord,' Grandma breathed, choking a little, but her own cough was becoming second nature to her.

'I'll wet another piece. If we keep it damp, it should filter out enough soot so she can breathe,' Grandpa said reasonably, but his eyes were glistening.

'You're a brilliant man, you know that?' Grandma whispered.

'Ah,' he protested, but she knew he was pleased at the praise, and even more relieved that his precious new granddaughter now had a fighting chance at life.

It was years before they told La Wanda the story of her first smoky hours of life.

Frowning, she drew in her shoulders, picturing herself in a narrow cardboard box covered with damp cheesecloth collecting soot before it could enter her tiny lungs.

'No wonder I'm claustrophobic,' she laughed. But she hugged her grandparents. 'Small price to pay.'

'If the whole house had burned down, it still would have been a small price to pay for our girl. Your cradle smoked,' her grandmother laughed, 'and you haven't slowed down since.'

BABE OF THE WOODS ☙

She'd been 'Mom' for as long as I could remember, though I knew her husband wasn't my father. Daddy used to come and pick up me and my older sister nearly every weekend and take us home to his farm. He was fresh-washed, his leathery skin scrubbed raw, but his stubble chafed our faces and his jacket smelled of pines and dust and cedar and sweat as we ran to be pressed into overwhelming warm darkness in his arms.

Each weekend Dad worked his farm with the same strength and gusto he'd worked all week in the woods. We 'helped' him chop and hoe and scrub and sweep and tie back and free and cook. I mostly helped with the dishes because when they were done and the table was cleared for the evening, Kate and Dad and I sat down to checkers or hangman or snuggled into his lap, all three of us in the squeaky wooden rocker, while he read to us about magic carpets and beautiful princesses and handsome young adventurers who swept them away into happily-ever-after.

Monday morning Dad would gather us up and drive us to Mom's farm just in time to catch the long yellow bus to school. There were few weekends when Dad couldn't come for us. He had trap lines, so Mom told us, and sometimes he had to be out walking the lines and gathering pelts.

'I can walk on lines,' I protested. 'Why can't I go with him?' But I knew there was a reason, because unless there was a very, very good one, Daddy always came for us.

I was six, a big girl now. It was a Friday, I know, because Kate and I had packed all our stuff the night before. We ran giggling from the bus stop, flinging ourselves into Mom's kitchen. Kate stopped. I almost plowed into her, I was so anxious to jump into Daddy's arms.

'Hey,' I protested, skirting around her to the tall man with the broad shoulders who was standing turned mostly away from us.

I slowed. There was another man, also tall and heavy shouldered, with dark features and narrowed eyes a little like my daddy's. Neither man spoke.

I ran to Mom, but she was crying as she gathered Kate and me into her arms. She said words that made no sense. Daddy wasn't coming. No, he wasn't waiting at our farm. He wasn't out on his trap lines. He wasn't coming for us because he couldn't.

'Whadda ya mean, he can't come ever? He'll be here next weekend. He'll be here, just you wait and see!' I informed them all.

The big men were my uncles, Daddy's brothers. Mom helped tuck us into their pickup truck. I reached up to touch her wet cheek and stared at the glistening on my fingertips while Kate clung to her. Uncle Henry peeled her gently away and settled her in his arms while Uncle Dan drove. They took us to their mother's.

Grandma was fierce. We'd only been with her a few months. We'd begun to make friends at the school near her house and Billy and Suzie Mae stood beside me flat-footed and open-mouthed on the sidewalk when we saw the sheriff's car in Grandma's driveway.

Grandma burst out onto the porch, clutching Kate and trying to get to me, but the sheriff held her gently by the shoulders and talked and talked to her in a low voice like Grandma used to rock us to sleep. Kate was crying. I started to run, but a skinny man with pimples on his neck and a lady in a blue skirt and a scratchy metal star pinned to her blue blouse caught me. The lady drew me into her arms and held me so I couldn't get away. She smelled like violets, like a whole bunch of violets, but her voice was soft and I was glad she was the one hugging me instead of the pimply man. He smelled like garlic.

They got us into the back of the police car, the lady holding me, and Kate by the other back door in the lap of the pimply garlic man. Grandma kept crying by the window and trying to get to us. The sheriff hugged her, telling her over and over that they were only divorced and she had a right. 'You know she's got the right, now. She's their mother.'

I never called her 'Mom.' I knew who Mom was and it wasn't this lady. But after a long time I found other names - Mums and Ma and others that she seemed to like - and we got along pretty good. Kate loved her, but I wasn't so sure. She kept telling me that Daddy wasn't ever going to be able to come back, but I knew she was lying.

She got the others, too, to tell me that some logs had shifted in their load. Uncle Dan tried to explain about how logs roll under their straps. That they are big and heavy and can go so fast even my daddy wasn't quick enough to get out of the way, but I knew they were all lying. My daddy was coming back for me someday as soon as he could.

I was ten, and there he was, standing on the staircase with the light from the window behind him so his tall frame and big shoulders loomed huge and dark, just like I remembered.

'Daddy!' I screamed and ran. I launched myself into his arms and he caught me and hugged me in the cedar and pines and dust darkness of his jacket.

But when I lifted my face to wipe my nose and streaming eyes with the back of my hand, it wasn't Daddy who was looking at me with eyes of love, but Uncle Henry.

'Hi, Half-pint,' he whispered and started to set me down until he saw my face. He hugged me for real then. A long time, while I sobbed.

I grew up, met a gentle giant who wooed and married me and gave me children of my own. He loved them as I loved them and Daddy had loved us. We had our ups and downs, of course, and money was always a problem. It usually is for those who rely on timber for their living. But we prospered as a family. My children called 'Mom' Nanna and my mother 'Nanny,' and that suited us all.

I was thirty and hiking with the family on a trail to an overlook above the Columbia River Gorge. My kids had run ahead with the exuberance and lusty lungs of youth. Uncle Henry was just ahead of me when we reached the edge of the clearing and he paused to half-turn back to me. The sunlight was behind him. It silhouetted his tall figure and broad shoulders and I stopped, zinged as though by an electric shock.

He must have heard my gasp because he turned full around and stepped toward me, taking my arm and peering into my face, his dark eyes narrowed with concern. He was coatless, but the woods around us smelled of cedar and pine and dust and love.

'You're so much like my father,' I murmured when I could.

'Thank you,' he whispered, his eyes, too, brimming with tears.

LOG ROLL ◆

A man needs a fine sense of irony to remain in logging.

When Hugh's brother is rolled over by a forty-eight foot tree being felled, his bride-to-be knows she doesn't want her Hugh to continue working in the woods.

So he smiles and agrees and goes to work in the sawmill. Only just before the wedding, one of his co-workers is accidentally knocked onto the moving logs. Before the mechanism can be stopped or the man dragged away, he is carried under the saws. It is more than a case of split personality.

The bride-to-be stamps her foot - both feet. Timber work of any kind is simply too dangerous. She doesn't want to end up as a young widow. And she doesn't relish the idea of a lifetime caring for a man maimed in the woods. Ultimatum: If you want to marry me, there'll be no working in or around the woods or associated occupation.

Well, he doesn't know any other kind of work. It's what he's been doing all his life. But Hugh is young. He loves his gal and he's willing to learn.

Hugh becomes a butcher. It's steady work. He's good at it. They are married and all set to live happily ever after.

Only Hugh begins to itch. He develops rashes. Hugh develops allergies to something about his butchering business. As he sits down on his new sofa to cuddle his bride, he ends up scratching his own arms and shoulders, and his back, his legs. Something has to be done.

Hugh goes into construction work. He likes working outdoors again. He likes working with the heavy equipment and the skilled and nonchalantly brave men on his crew. He enjoys again the camaraderie he had when he worked in the woods. His wife is satisfied that he is happy, a good provider, but in less danger than he was when he was a logger or a sawmill worker.

She smiles as she hands him his lunch pail and kisses him good-bye for another day on the job.

Only this day Hugh lets himself down into the deep sewer ditch they are constructing. The walls of the ditch collapse and bury him alive.

A logger needs a fine sense of irony when he tries to leave the woods, too.

HOME PLACE

I know about kids. I've got 98 kids, grandkids, great and great, great grandkids. I'd like to have a hundred, but it looks like they all quit on me. Not sure I'll be around by the time the newest generation start having their kids. I'm 87 years old now.

We came from Oklahoma. We lived in Hillsboro, Oregon, a short time, then we moved out to the farm on the Old Wilson River Road.

The place was pretty well stripped of most of its timber when we got it. But we was here fifty years, and the timber re-grew.

We moved into a two-story house that had been built in 1904. It was in pretty good shape, but the mortar was more worn away between the bricks in the chimney than we knew.

One day, about 1943, we had a real good hailstorm. It hailed so hard that the rest of the mortar got carried away. We had a fire going, not realizing sparks was going right up the chimney and out between the bricks to the roof. The roof caught on fire, and we barely had enough time to get us all out. Nearly everything we had was gone in that fire.

Floyd was building a new chicken house. It was made of new lumber. Floyd just added on, and we moved in. Over the years we added on more. But that original chicken house still is the bedrooms and the hallway.

Years later John and Bessie got ambitious and built on one more bedroom.

You could say we pulled ourselves up by our own bootstraps.

To Faye Stuck

BIG FOOT DEL

Death information is usually not given out over the police radio. Too many people are listening. And the next-of-kin need the comfort and caring of another person when they receive notice a loved one has died - or been killed.

But no law enforcement officer wants the duty of notification. Jurisdiction becomes very finely adhered to in these cases.

The teen-ager died playing basketball in Multnomah County, Oregon. Of course, it was Multnomah County that investigated the death. Their medical examiner then called Washington County and asked them to deliver the death message as the mother lived in Washington County. The Multnomah County medical examiner sighed, at least partly in relief, as he hung up the phone.

Washington County dispatch sent Del a message: 'Officer Konschu, 10-21.'

His gray-green eyes narrowing under their straight, brown brows, Del acknowledged into his patrol car's microphone and pulled to the end of the block. There was a telephone booth two streets over. One thing about patrolling, you get to know the features of your neighborhood. Your life could depend on that knowledge in a split-second. Those who don't take the time and attention to learn sometimes wish - fleetingly - that they had.

But as Del turned the corner, he wondered why he'd been ordered to call in to Dispatch on a land line. What kind of message would it be? And how would he like standing there in the lighted glass-walled booth for all to see how he reacted when he got that message?

Del was on night duty in the area of Washington County that is north of Highway 8 and east of Cedar Hills Boulevard, so he turned again at the next intersection and headed to the Cedar Mill Fire Department to make the call. They'd give him a private area. And if worse came to worst, they'd be fellow professionals who would help and support him if he needed them.

He pulled in and parked. The station chief quickly sent him to his own office to use his phone.

'Del, I'm sorry,' the dispatcher, Sue, told him, 'but there's been a death and someone needs to notify the next of kin.'

Del let his breath out slowly. That was bad, but at least it wasn't his own family. He blinked. That is what he'd been so afraid of, he realized.

'Okay,' he said softly. It wasn't a burden he wanted to carry, but it came with the job. If he'd been in such sweaty palmed anxiety over his Pam and the girls, at least he was geared up to have empathy for the poor soul he'd have to face in a few minutes. Another traffic accident, probably. There were so many, and so sudden - no warning. No way to begin to cope, and, smash, a life, a love, was gone.

'...the mother lives here in Washington County, off Thompson Road.'

'The mother?' Del asked, knowing that his mind had blanked out something.

The dispatcher gave him her name and address. 'Too bad,' she said. 'He was only a teen-ager, playing basketball. He just collapsed and died and there was nothing they could do. It's going to be a tough one, Del. I'm sorry.'

Sue was far too tender sometimes to be in the gut-wrenching position she was in. But Del knew she was incredibly sharp and tenacious in an emergency.

'Thanks,' Del whispered. He sat unmoving after hanging up the phone. A teenager? Lord, this was really bad. Del bowed his head a moment asking for strength. And compassion.

It took all his strength to rise. The station chief waited quietly by the nearest engine. He raised unruly eyebrows.

'My family's okay,' Del said, grateful for the concern. 'But it's a death notification.'

The chief's eyebrows knitted into a hedgerow. 'Those are tough,' he said, shaking his head.

'Yeah,' Del breathed and nodded thank you. He couldn't tell him that this was a teenager. Or that this was Del's first death notification. He was glad that someone was going to do this personally - not by telephone. But he wasn't glad that that someone was Del Konschu.

It was nearly midnight when he got to the white bungalow. The lights were still on. A large patch of yellow light from the glass panels beside the front door showed neat gray-painted trim. The knob was worn brass. A pointed brass knocker and plate hung just off-center, but Del closed his hand into a fist and knocked. Somehow it seemed important to physically be in touch with the pain he was bringing to this family.

The door was answered almost immediately. The short, round-faced, middle-aged woman pulled back the door only far enough for her to stand full in its aperture.

'Yes?' she said, then her hazel eyes widened as she took in Del's uniform. He was a foot and a half taller than she was. He could see her eyes move up until they met his gaze.

'I've got something important to tell you,' Del said quietly. 'Could we please step inside?'

But she wouldn't move an inch. She seemed rooted to the doorsill. 'What is it? Something's wrong, isn't it?'

'Please, Ma'am, it would be better if we went inside.'

Del tried every opening he could think of, but nothing would get her to move out of the doorway. Finally, he took a deep breath and told her what had happened.

'He was playing basketball.'

'Yes, I knew he was at the gym. He should have been home more than an hour ago. If he's going to be late, he always finds some way to call so I won't be worried. He's a good boy. He can't be in any trouble with the police!'

'No, Ma'am,' Del said. 'I'm sure he is - was - a very good boy.'

The woman's eyes went huge. 'Wh- what?'

'Your son - your son collapsed on the basketball court, Ma'am.'

'Collapsed? He's hurt?'

'Please, Ma'am, can't we go inside? I hate to tell you this out here on the porch.'

'Something's happened to my Tommy? My Tommy boy is hurt?' Her voice rose, thinning toward piercing. 'Where is he? Is he at the hospital? Did they take Tommy to the hospital?'

'Please, Ma'am,' Del begged.

'Tell me! Where's my boy? Where's Tommy? You said he collapsed. Is he...? Oh, God, is Tommy...?'

Del could only nod. 'The Multnomah County Medical Examiner reported that he died right there. There was nothing anyone could do. It all happened too fast. They couldn't revive him.'

Del's words seemed to slam into her, though he'd tried so hard to find a gentle way. Her face twisted in grief and her knees buckled. Del lunged forward to catch her in his arms. He bent to support her shoulders and she tottered there, barely staying upright. He could feel her sobs wracking her body. Her cries began low, but were rising higher and higher. Del had seen hysteria before. He knew he needed to get her somewhere where she could sit or lie down.

Del tried to shove the door wider with his shoulder. 'Please, Ma'am, I've got to get you inside.' He was beginning to breathe hard; more and more of her weight was collapsing into his arms. She didn't budge an inch. 'Please, Ma'am, why don't we go into the house?'

Her sobs grew louder, but somewhere between them she managed, 'I can't move. You're standing on my foot.'

'Oh, Lord,' Del breathed, cursing his own ineptitude. But he didn't let go. Somehow, his foot moved from on top of hers, he was able to lift and guide her into the living room, where he helped her collapse on the sofa. He got a number from her and called a close friend to come immediately to be with her. The woman was there within minutes, and between them they were able to call family members to come.

Del stood to one side of the entry hall, answering what questions he could. He gave a man - presumably the woman's brother, uncle to the dead boy - the official information so they could contact Multnomah County. At last the house was filling with grieving relatives. The mother would be cared for. Del nodded to her and to her brother and slipped away out the front door.

He scuffed the doorsill, berating himself for a clumsy fool.

'Smart move, Konschu,' he breathed as he walked out to his patrol car. 'Your first death notification and you screwed up, but good. How could you do such a stupid thing as step on the woman's foot? Couldn't you feel it under your shoe?'

He didn't forgive himself until the teenager's service, which he attended quietly, staying in the background. He was about to slip away without saying anything, when the uncle walked up and offered his hand.

'You're the tall man with the kind eyes. You're the officer who came to the door to tell my sister what happened, aren't you?'

Self-consciously, Del lifted his foot and stepped backward. 'Yes, I came to notify your family. I'm so sorry.'

'Thank you. My sister saw you and asked me to tell you how grateful we are for the way you handled what had to have been a tough situation for you, too. She asked me to thank you for your strength and your gentleness.'

'And my big feet?'

The man, grief-stricken, broke into a smile, probably the first his face had felt in days. 'She - she told me about that. She said it was probably the only thing that held her up.' He shook Del's hand again. 'Thank you for being the one who came, big feet and all.'

PASSAGE ✝

'She's so old,' Mandy grimaced. 'Her skin is so wrinkled and all those creases above her lip. They always have those ugly puckered lips on witches when they draw them.'

'We'll get them, too, little sister mine. And the only way you can get rid of them is to grin. Do you think the Lord is trying to tell us something with that one? Something about taking old age with a deepening sense of humor.' Ann smiled, but her younger sister's active hands were clenched at her sides. Mandy, who could still run a fifty-yard dash without breaking much of a sweat, had a line of moisture on her upper lip.

'It's Aunt Marie, Mand,' Ann said quietly. 'She's ninety one.'

'I know that. She's been ancient since I can remember.' Mandy shook her head, looking around the foyer of the nursing home.

'I don't remember that being a problem for you before.' Ann stopped to one side to let a gaunt man totter past them, head-down, leaning into his walker. A gray-haired woman who filled in the width of her wheelchair grunted as she worked the control fastened to the chair's tubular right arm.

'Sorry,' Mandy muttered, and Ann couldn't be sure whom she was more sorry for, the woman she'd inadvertently blocked or herself for being there to do the blocking.

It was on the tip of Ann's tongue to say, 'Well, if you feel that way, why don't you wait in the car,' but something held her back. She closed her mouth with the distinct impression that someone was telling her not to interfere.

'Interfere?' Mandy glanced at her with raised eyebrows, those animated hazel eyes questioning. Ann must have said the word aloud.

'I think we're interrupting the traffic flow here in the lobby,' Ann said, striding toward the east hall, toward Aunt Marie's room. She didn't look back. She couldn't shake the feeling that this visit was important both for their precious mother's oldest sister and for her own youngest sister. She didn't dare make eye contact now for fear of somehow giving Mandy a way to escape.

'Come on, Mandy,' Ann whispered, willing the dark-haired fireball of a younger sister to follow her. There was something to be done here, something to be learned. Ann murmured a quick prayer that she would have the insight to know what to do and what to say.

Ann had come to see Aunt Marie every week or so in the past few months. The elderly sprite of a woman always greeted her like the daughter she'd lost years ago.

But today was indeed different. Ann halted in the doorway, catching her breath.

'Aunt Marie?' Ann called low, almost hoping the old woman was too far gone into sleep to hear her. The stoop-shouldered, laughing woman who had wrapped her in such love since childhood had looked frail this past year. But today, she was wasted, gray, and shriveled. It wasn't only her upper lip that was puckered and - well, face it - ugly. The sleeping figure was pitiable, almost repulsive, except to someone who loved her.

Ann heard Mandy's sharp heel-strikes on the tile-on-cement foundation hall. How could she let Mandy see Aunt Marie this way? How could she protect the memories, keep them from being spoiled by this sight that would crowd out the mental pictures of fun and loving family times together?

Ann lifted her hand to motion to Mandy not to come, but a croaking voice called her.

'Ann? Ann, dear, is that you?'

Dropping her hand, Ann stepped into the narrow room. 'Hello, Aunt Marie. Yes, it's me. How are you?' Ann said. No matter what the figure on the bed looked like, the voice said it was Aunt Marie and Ann couldn't do anything but respond to the love she had been given since she could toddle to those arms.

Ann sat down in the straight chair beside the bed and was taking up the white, bony hand when Mandy reached the doorway. Ann heard her gasp, felt the panic in her breathing, saw the stiffness as her little sister poised, ready to run.

'Come in, Mandy,' Ann heard her own voice say calmly. It was more than merely welcome, but something less than an order. It was direction, and Mandy entered as though the voice had drawn her when she was powerless to do anything but what she was told. 'Come and sit here by me,' Ann told her sister softly.

Carrying the second straight chair over to set it so Ann was between her and the body on the bed, Mandy did sit down. Her brown eyes were filling with tears so the green flecks glistened.

'It's Mandy, Aunt Marie,' Ann said. 'She's come to visit you, too.'

'Ah, Mandy.' the croaking voice broke trying to say her name.

Mandy sat rigid in the chair. At that moment, nothing could have induced her to look at her aunt - or anything else.

'Easy, Love,' Ann whispered, though to tell the truth, she wanted so much to escape that she couldn't blame Mandy for wanting to, too.

Ann took a deep breath and let it out slowly with her lips pursed. Mandy, who recognized their Tae Kwan Do master's technique for regaining control, lifted her chin. All right, her stricken doe eyes told Ann, I'll try. Her shoulders rose and she took in a deliberate breath. She shuddered, but gamely drew in another breath and let it out, then a third, a deep one, and held it a moment with her eyes closed. When she let it out again with pursed lips, Ann could see her sister's natural grace emerge from the stiffness.

Grace. Amazing grace. Ann felt the music fill her. Music had always given expression to her soul. 'Amazing Grace,' she crooned, a lullaby to both her sister and her aunt. And to herself. 'Amazing grace... that saved a wretch like me.' Grace for a woman who couldn't face walking into the room where her own beloved aunt was suffering alone. 'And grace my fears relieved...'

'How precious did that grace appear...' Mandy's firm contralto joined Ann's sweet melody. Ann glanced over at her, her own eyes brimming with tears. '... The hour I first believed.'

Aunt Marie's shoulders eased into the base of her pillow. She took a sighing breath and, as she let it out, lay more quietly on the bed. Like Mandy, the rigid muscles let go their stiff attempts at control, and she turned toward them onto her side like a child curling toward peaceful sleep.

'Through many dangers,' Marie whispered, her voice dry, not even trying for song, merely a desire to be part of this moment with her nieces. To acknowledge their gift of belonging - to them, and to the Lord.

As the sisters sang, they watched the elderly woman close her eyes. A tear eased between the lids and slid over the hollow cheekbone to the pillow. Ann's voice caught. She swallowed back a sob. It was the younger sister who picked up the third verse. 'Through many dangers, toils and snares...' Mandy sang with a husky richness Ann had never heard in her voice before.

'I have already come,' Ann joined her and Mandy slipped down in harmony. They studied the wizened form on the bed beside them. Mandy drew her chair to one side, closer to the bed. She laid her own hand gently on her aunt's other wasted one.

'Already come,' Marie mouthed. Her fingers closed around Mandy's pinkie the way a baby clutches the loving finger that strokes it.

'You've fought so long and so well, Aunt Marie,' Ann told her quietly. 'You've lived a life of love and fun and giving to all us kids for a couple generations now and we love you for it. You've shown us that the Lord's way is a way of joy, despite the hardships and the pain. Thank you.'

'...brought me safe...' Marie whispered. 'Oh, Lord, You've always... I didn't know, Lord...didn't understand.' Her eyes opened wide. The milky cataracts blazoned with a sheen of fear that would have terrified the sisters only minutes ago. But now Mandy stroked the blue veins in the back of her aunt's hand. Ann leaned closer.

'None of us understands, Aunt Marie,' Ann said, knowing it was true. 'We all fall short - so short of what we know we should be. We do things... Wasn't it St. Paul himself that lamented how often he did the things he shouldn't? And didn't do the things he knew he should? If Paul, who had heard the Lord speak directly to him, if Paul couldn't measure up, then we can't either.'

'That's why we need Grace,' Mandy said, stroking her aunt's limp hair away from her face. 'We can't earn it.'

'It's a gift from God who loves us more deeply than we could ever imagine, let alone be worthy of.'

'God loves us even more than you did, Auntie Marie,' Mandy laughed that wonderful, little girl laugh that had charmed Mandy's way out of most of the trouble that same spirit had gotten her into. 'And He loves you to the top of the sky!'

They sat for a long time, two grateful sisters holding the hand of the woman who had loved them. Ann and Mandy wept, for loss, for sadness, for hope and joy.

'...lead me home...' Ann whispered.

Mandy cleared her throat gently and picked up the moving melody.

"'Tis grace hath brought me safe thus far, And grace will lead me home,' the sisters sang with a sweet richness despite the quiet of their voices.

Marie lay quiet. Mandy sat back, sobbing, until Ann drew her sister's head onto her own shoulder. Her own tears flowed unchecked down her cheeks. Gradually she withdrew her hand from Aunt Marie's lifeless one and encircled her sister's shoulders.

'He's led her home, Mandy,' Ann whispered. 'He's led her home.'

For JoAnn

TATTERED

Gusts flutter the corners of that macabre piece of hope. The wind is not more merciful than the man in the silver sports car. Rain falls on the just and the unjust, and wind ruffles the hair of the survivors, as I'm sure it does the killer. If only she knew who he was.

I don't know what I'm proving, standing here in the deserted parking lot at dawn, looking at her naive plea tacked to the telephone pole. She was so sure that if people knew what really happened, they would help. So she wrote out her gut-twistingly simple description of what happened, had the page reprinted a hundred times or more, and went out tacking and taping and handing out to anyone who would let her.

I tried to point out that whoever killed Bobby was a person, too, so what could she expect? But she snapped at me: 'He's not a human being. He's sick or an addict.

He doesn't deserve God's love. I only know he has it, and there is nothing I can do about that. I just know most people are good, Sammy. Most people will be as appalled as we are and they'll help us.'

I read and reread her scrawled words as the wind flattens them and then tears them from my vision: Accident. Bobby (so young to die) hurt on this Interstate 5 Highway (that the gods of speed and greed have used for decades to cull those destined to be their sacrificial lambs) south of Sacramento (and just far enough north of the cattle feed lots to be free of the stench unless the wind blows stiffly from the south. It often does.)

It wasn't much of an accident. Bobby was hurt. Passers-by and restaurant patrons had shoved his car ahead to the side of the highway out of danger's way. Gentle if unskilled hands had laid him out on a woman's crocheted afghan as she hurried with it to them from this restaurant. She'd seen what happened and ran to get it from her car here in the parking lot.

He was bleeding. She said, 'Never mind. We can't put him on the ground. If the blood washes out, it washes out. Otherwise...' She shrugged and helped wipe his face with a white hanky from her purse.

They say he even tried to smile at her. He couldn't talk yet, but he knew and he tried to smile. Someone had already called the police from Bologna Joe's here.

One of the men who had helped push Bobby's car looked back to see if the ambulance was coming. 'Holy Jehosaphat,' he muttered half out loud.

The others, embarrassed to stand there but not wanting to leave, looked where he was staring.

'Lord Almighty! He must be dr...'

That's all there was time for.

The silver sports car (they couldn't agree on what kind) came weaving south. One older man ambled forward, beyond Bobby. If he hadn't started the movement, maybe they'd all have been struck down like ten pins.

In the end the silver streak weaved or turned deliberately to its right. One of the men hauled up the lady with the handkerchief and flung her into the ditch. He jumped after her, just in time. The others scattered the best way they could and came up with bruises from the sports car or their falls. None of them could believe what had just happened. None of them could even look.

They'd all fled but Bobby. He couldn't move out of the way and no one had time to rescue him.

No one could fight the shock enough to look for a license plate number. They stood or lay or crouched where they'd been scattered, trying hard to concentrate on breathing. The woman pressed her bloody handkerchief against her mouth and moaned.

The police had two ambulances come and fetch corpse and near-victims (most by then back at the restaurant, groaning and crying over hot coffee, compliments of Joe.)

The wind is flipping her letter and plea so fast now I can't read it any more, but I couldn't anyway. My eyes are brimming tears. I can't walk. But I'm going to. As soon as I can. I'm going to walk across this parking lot and stand again on that shoulder of the road. I have to, to be sure I remember.

I want to go on with life, with my life at least. But I have to remember what she is feeling - still. I have to remember so I can see the blank eyes and not be peeved that so much of her is still here, with Bobby.

"It will help," I whisper to her on that merciless wind. "Someone will see your note. Maybe we'll never know about Bobby, but maybe someone will know to park his car at the side of the road to protect the next victim. People are good, Love. Most people are good, like the lady with the afghan and the guy who heaved her into the ditch..."

'At least it was only Bobby,' she told me just before her eyes went dim. She'd hoped.

It just took too long.

THE COURAGE OF HOPE ✝

Shawn stood half-in and half-out at the doorway. 'Hi, Mom,' he managed before the scowl took over.

'So, come in,' Carol said, pointing to the chair across from her at the small kitchen table. 'Glad you could come.'

He raised his hands as though pleading. 'If it's bad news...'

'I'd get it over with,' she said. 'No, not bad news. No news, really, I just wanted to see my only son.'

Shawn slouched forward to lounge against the new cabinet and counter top. 'I see Buster's been busy for you again. The lighter wood makes the whole place a lot more open and bright.'

'Did you see in the garden? He's got the pond all set up. Probably get the waterfall working by this weekend.'

'It looks great, Mom. I can't believe what you two have done with this place over the years.'

'It was a mess when we got it,' Carol tossed her full, dark hair and chuckled. 'But to tell you the truth I didn't see any of that. The mire where the kid had torn up the ground with his three-wheeler. The filth, even inside. These druggies aren't known as good housekeepers, I guess.'

'He lived like a pig. It turned me completely off the place when I saw it.'

'I guess Buster thought I was crazy, too, but all I saw was what it could be.'

Shawn almost smiled then, but his eyes were clouding over.

'Hey,' Carol said sharply. 'I didn't want you here for that, you know. I not only don't want your pity, it hurts me. Why do you think I sent away all of my friends who couldn't laugh with me?'

Shawn pushed away from the cabinet with his full shoulders. His chin jutted. 'So we all have to keep up appearances,' he muttered.

'No, we have to deal with the cancer.'

'I really try being good for you, laughing and all that, but sometimes the mask is too heavy...'

'Look at those shoulders on you. Twenty-nine years old and strong as a bull. But it isn't a mask, Shawn. Not for me, and not for you. Sit down here at my table.'

He did break into a fond smile then. 'So we're going to hash this out. Like when I was a kid.'

'Well, no one is going to get up from this table until we get this settled,' Carol admitted, and grinned. 'You remember.'

He raised thick eyebrows over those incredibly dark lashes and deep gray eyes. It made Carol's heart skip to watch that move of acceptance-under-protest that had warmed her heart when he was a child.

'How could a fellow forget being bullied by the peacemaker?' Shawn laughed and twisted the chair to straddle it and lean on its back looking at her.

A lump caught in her throat for a moment. Her eyes, too, filled with forbidden tears.

Shawn's frown flew back in that instant. 'There is more,' he said, half-rising involuntarily.

'No,' she shook her head and banished the tears, 'I was just remembering. You were such an adorable little mutt.'

'And now you're wondering what happened?'

She smiled. 'I know what happened, and I'm proud of every minute of it. You're a fine young man, Shawn. And you had to do most of that on your own.'

'Not completely,' he said quietly. 'Why do you think I haven't been coming around the way I used to? When Doctor O came to the surgery waiting room at the hospital this last time...'

Scowling, Carol willed her voice to stay quiet. 'What did he say, exactly?' she asked.

This time his tears threatened to spill onto his cheeks but he faced her. 'He said that you were filled with cancer and didn't have a prayer of living more than a couple months. He wanted us to help you get your affairs in order. I'm sorry, Mom, but this third time it was too much. I couldn't take any more. I ran away.'

'Rats!' she exhaled, trying hard not to curse the surgeon. 'Shawn, he didn't have the right to do that. It was wrong of him to take away all hope like that.'

'But it's true,' he shrugged, twisting on the wooden chair.

'How would he know when I'm going to die? Nobody knows, not for sure. When I go is up to the Big Guy. I could be dead in two months, or ten, or twenty-six years, or even fifty years. Nobody on this earth knows for sure. Shawn, listen to me. You could be in an accident on the way home today and die before I do.'

Shawn inhaled, his eyes wide. He let his breath out slowly. At twenty-nine, you don't think in those terms very often.

Her heart went out to him. She wanted to get up and run around the table to hold him in her arms and take back her words. But in the long run, that would be crueler than letting him face this thing head on. He had to grow up. There was no help for it and no putting it off.

'Nobody knows,' she whispered. 'It's up to the Big Guy. If I can face this, then you can, too.'

He took two deep breaths and faced her. 'I see what you mean. You're right, Mom. I'm sorry I've stayed away.'

'It's not about being right, or wrong. It's about getting to spend some time with you.'

His face drawn, he lifted his chin. 'Here I am,' he said quietly.

'Well, good. Come on, let's practice a couple songs before you have to go.' Carol rose, and Shawn came around the table. She wasn't sure she could hold up if he embraced her.

He was thinking about doing just that, she could tell. But he assessed her with that no-nonsense appraisal he'd developed as a kid. He knew. Shawn laughed and put his hand on her shoulder to walk with her into the living room to the old, upright piano.

Carol closed her eyes. It had been weeks since they'd sung together. She felt the tears welling, but brushed the back of her hand impatiently across her cheek. If Shawn had to face this without tears, then fair was fair. She had to, too. Sometimes her look-it-in-the-eye approach was tough, but it had proved to be the only way that worked. She needed to define where she wanted to be and then do what she had to do to get there. And right now she wanted to share an hour's music with her son. She smiled. No matter how many hours there were left on this earth, this was going to be one of the good ones.

GERRY DANCERS

He'd worked the long holiday weekend on the deck, so when his right shoulder hurt everyone was sure that he'd pulled a rarely used muscle.

'Just a little lineament and it'll be fine,' he told Pam. But then he couldn't let her rub it on. 'Boy, that's really tender,' he muttered, motioning her away with his left hand. He didn't sleep well Sunday night. Monday morning, Labor Day, he was in pain. Not his shoulder, but his abdomen.

'Pam, Honey, are you awake?'

She stirred, startled and afraid. His tone told her, even in her sleep, that Gerry was in trouble.

'Wha'? Gerry?' She turned toward him, but the jouncing of the bed made him grunt.

They spent all of Labor Day in the Emergency Room at the closest hospital. Over the next weeks and months, Pam sat in a lot of lobbies and waiting rooms, always as near to her husband as the staff would let her be.

The G.I. specialists were methodical and thorough. They put Gerry through each test and then the next. It was all so logical. It was all wrong, but they had no way to know that except hindsight.

At last, weeks of pain later, Pam drove Gerry home slowly from the hospital after his CAT scan and MRI. The trip took more than half an hour.

When they reached home, there was a phone message from the doctor: 'I'm waiting in your room at the Bremerton Hospital. Come immediately. There's a tumor on Gerry's spine. It's pressing on nerves that service the abdomen, hence the gut pain, but it hasn't anything to do with Gerry's G.I. system at all. But where it is on the spine, if it ruptures, it could paralyze him.'

After two days in the hospital in Bremerton, Gerry was transferred to Swedish Hospital in Seattle to the care of a surgeon so gifted and experienced that he was the one doctors chose if they or their families needed an operation.

'I know that Gerry has had a skin cancer removed,' the feisty surgeon assured them. 'Malignant melanoma is one of the nastiest and I'm sure you've thought, too, that this tumor on his spine could be metastasis from that. But in all my years of experience, I've never seen melanoma spread to the spine this way. Yes, Gerry's tumor could well be cancer, but I'll be surprised if it isn't another type than melanoma.'

Pam sat back, blinking. Another cancer?

The surgeon began to rise, and Pam stirred herself. She wanted to be absolutely sure that he realized how bony and stiff Gerry's back had grown over the years.

'Ankylosing spondylosis, yes, I know,' the surgeon assured her. 'This isn't the first time I've had to deal with that kind of rigidity of the spinal column either. I still believe that we can surgically remove Gerry's tumor and reduce, if not eliminate, the danger of its paralyzing him.'

He seemed so sure. He'd done so much.

Gerry and Pam agreed to the surgery. The alternative was a time bomb.

The operation usually lasted an hour and a half. Four hours after Gerry had been wheeled into the surgery suite, Pam was still sitting and waiting.

The surgeon came, finally, peeling off his mask and wiping his brow. 'I've done 800 of these and Gerry's was one of the toughest, and most unusual. The specimen we sent down to the lab from the operating room looked like melanoma.' He shook his head. 'I've never seen melanoma go to the spine. We'll wait and get definitive results in a couple days,' he added as though he were sure the later view of treated and stained tissue under the microscope would confirm his idea that the tumor was another cancer, not melanoma.

'The good news, Pam, is that Gerry is recovering nicely. He was able to move his toes for us, so there's hope for a good outcome from the surgery. We'll just have to deal with the tumor when we know for sure what it is and the best way to combat it.'

Pam exhaled slowly and extended her hand to thank him. There were too many emotions flooding through her to be able to express in words what she was feeling. The voluble surgeon smiled, wearily, but glad.

'We do what we can, Pam,' he said gently. 'We do what we have to.'

Pam knew he would be honest with her. When he turned away back to the restricted halls of the surgery wing, Pam sat down and cried. And prayed. And cried.

Gerry could move his toes after surgery. Gerry was learning to shuffle, trying to relearn to walk. He worked hard under Physical Therapy's astute guidance. And then one day he lost the use of both legs.

And the pain returned. Unbearable pain that the staff couldn't seem to control.

Pathology returned the unthinkable verdict: the tumor on Gerry's spine was malignant melanoma.

Gerry was to return to the care of his oncologist. He was looking forward to going back to Bremerton.

Pam sat by the elevator, figuring that the transfer team had to come up that way. She didn't want to miss them. There were 10,000 flowers in Gerry's room and all his things had been packed up for hours as they waited for a bed to be available across the Puget Sound.

'Mrs. Duvall? I think they're moving your husband now. Right now,' a nurse informed her. The transfer team had come up the back way.

'What? Oh.'

The room was empty of Gerry but none of his things.

'We'll have to leave all that to you, I guess,' the paramedic told her in the hallway. 'If we don't go right this minute, we'll miss the ferry across the sound to Bremerton. If we miss that, it'll be hours waiting with him.'

'Oh,' Pam cried. 'I'm coming with you. All these flowers. All his things... My friend is coming this evening. She'll take care of all of it. Leave it for her.' Pam gave the nurses quick instructions as she hurried down the hallway. (Pam's friend was startled - shocked, really - when she arrived. But she took care of everything, grateful to really be able to be of help.)

They loaded Gerry into the back of the ambulance and helped Pam up on the passenger's seat in front. 'We aren't gonna make that ferry,' the attendant predicted, glancing at his watch.

'We're going to give it one good try,' the driver said. He leaned forward to switch on the siren and revolving lights.

They barreled, screaming, through Seattle. They called ahead. Pam never knew who was backed off the ferry to make room for them, but the boat took off as soon as they were aboard and the gate secured behind them.

It was a glorious day. Gerry and Pam, holding hands, watched the receding skyline of Seattle through the open back door of the ambulance. It was the last time Gerry saw Seattle and it was a worthy farewell.

They were months in the hospital in Bremerton. They came to know everyone on the staff and joke and laugh with each of them. Gerry was like that. He'd always been a people person. He couldn't use his legs, so the staff rigged a trapeze above his bed so he could haul himself up on that to move or shift position.

And then that right shoulder - where all the pain had started in the first place while he was working on the deck - became so tender, he found he could no longer stand to use his right arm to pull himself up. Tests revealed another tumor. Also melanoma. Also malignant.

He was reduced to hoisting himself with his left arm only.

Their daughter-in-law brought in a toy stuffed monkey to keep him company on the trapeze.

He grinned. 'What I really need for this circus is a couple of dancing girls,' he muttered.

Pam looked across to their visiting friends. 'Oh, really?' she asked with wide, innocent eyes.

That night at dinner at a nearby restaurant, the three of them shared a glass of wine and plotted. A variety store was open. There were no dance costumes, but there were rolls of netting in various colors.

'I will if you will,' her friend said and she and Pam bought yards of vivid orange-pink.

It would have been funny anyway, but the glass of wine did make it easier. The two women shed much of their sedate clothing in the ladies room and wrapped each other in yards of hot pink like Hawaiian sunset clouds.

It was nearly the end of the day. Few visitors still remained on the hospital floor when Pam and her cohort emerged from the restroom, giggling.

The staff raised eyebrows and grins, but did nothing to stop them. In fact, many found reasons to be at the Duvall end of the corridor when Gerry's dancers made their grand entrance into his room.

'You asked for this, remember,' Pam admonished when her husband's mouth dropped open at the sight of them.

'I forgot. You have to be careful what you wish for, don't you?' he murmured, shaking his head and then the trapeze and bed in waves of deepening hilarity. 'I could die laughing with you two around.'

T ROSES

The two men spoke quietly so they wouldn't disturb T's hospital roommate.

"So, after you left your position as chief of police here in Eugene, you joined the United Nations?" Ed asked his blind and gravely ill friend.

"No, I went to work for the federal government, the Foreign Service Agency, helping other countries upgrade their police forces."

"I knew you two had lived in Greece and Brazil," Ed said. "And I seem to remember that you were in Libya, too - or was it Liberia?"

"Both," T chuckled.

"Jet-setters, huh? Paris? London? Monaco?" Ed teased.

"Hardly! We worked mainly in Third World countries plagued by coups and chaos where police forces hadn't been able to protect the lives of innocent citizens: Guam, El Salvador, Panama, Colombia, British Guiana, South Vietnam."

"And Lita went with you to all those places?"

"Not only did she go with me, she absolutely charmed the people. Invited them to our home for dinner. Made deep friendships. We still get Christmas cards from all over the world," T said.

"I see."

"Ed, she's been the best part of my life. Every step of the way, she's been right there, and she's been at my bedside with the heart attacks and the strokes. She even cuts up the meat on my plate now that I can't see it any more. She leads me back when I get lost going from our dining room to the living room. And she does it without sneering or acting like she's getting tired of the old man."

"Yeah, I remember after your last stroke, we couldn't make heads or tails out of what you were saying. But Lita knew."

"So you understand then..."

"I understand, T. I understand."

At three in the morning, Lita finally stumbled home from the hospital. Drained, she sat at the edge of their bed to take off her shoes and then fell back, too exhausted to undress or even to crawl under the covers.

She slept until after ten o'clock that morning - waking for the first time in a world without T. Just when he had finally begun to rally after his most recent heart attack, another massive stroke did him in. It had taken both calamities to still that strong-willed and tough, but gentle, man.

It took Lita two hours to leave their bed, so empty now without him, knowing he'd never return to her side. Weeping under a cascade of warm water, she felt refreshed enough after the shower to get dressed and get moving. She got as far as the living room and drew the blinds before sitting down in the shadows.

Reluctantly, she reached for the envelope T had left on the coffee table between their chairs. He'd given her strict instructions to open it once he was gone. The sight of her name written in the awkward, uphill letters he had reverted to when his vision faded tore at her heart. With trembling fingers, she eased the paper out of the envelope and was surprised to see the clarity of the handwriting, to see that it was not T's. Though the letters looked familiar, she couldn't place who had written this for him. But the squiggled signature at the bottom was definitely her husband's.

Sighing, Lita started to read what looked to be a list. And then she burst out in laughter. T had been at peace with what was happening and he had told her so, as he always had, in humor.

The list began: "If my body is to be cremated, make sure I'm really dead first."

The rest was a compilation of reminders of important papers and items that he wanted her to see to. This was followed by a detailed outline of his funeral service. It was so like him to take on the burden of the planning, to ease her sorrow now. He had requested a service of simple dignity, but one laced with the sardonic humor that he'd always used to deal with tough situations.

The tears again rose of themselves, and just then, there was a light rap at her front door. "Oh, no," she thought. It was too soon. She didn't feel up to facing anyone. Lita's first thought was to pretend she wasn't home. Then, hastily wiping her eyes, she took a deep breath and rose to look between the slats of the blinds.

Outside, she saw Ed's canary-yellow Beetle parked at the curb, and then Ed scurrying down the front walk.

"Ed!" she called from the door, but he merely waved.

"You okay?" he called.

She nodded. Ed waved again and got into his VW and drove away.

A long, white florist's box stood propped against the doorframe. It was tied with gold-edged red ribbon like the one T had sent her on their anniversary.

Lita felt the tears again as she brought the box into the house and closed the door.

She fumbled with the ribbon, unwilling to cut it with scissors. At last it slid off the end of the box, and she lifted the lid to look inside at a dozen perfect, long stemmed white roses. Nestled against the white satin ribbon was a tiny card with scrawled letters she could barely decipher. It was her husband's handwriting.

"Thanks," it said. "Love, T"

Do you have a story of
QUIET COURAGE ?

We'd love to hear from you

To tell us True stories that have happened to you or someone you know

Or to order copies of this first edition of QUIET COURAGE ($7.95 plus $2 P/H)

Mail us at:

TAWK Press
P.O. Box 974
Forest Grove, OR 97116

Or contact us at TAWKPress.com